His Mercy Endures Forever

His Mercy Endures Forever

Biblical Reflections on Divine Mercy for Anytime

Psalm 136:1

MARK G. BOYER

WIPF & STOCK · Eugene, Oregon

HIS MERCY ENDURES FOREVER
Biblical Reflections on Divine Mercy for Anytime

Copyright © 2024 Mark G. Boyer. All rights reserved. Except for brief quotations in critical publications or reviews, no part of this book may be reproduced in any manner without prior written permission from the publisher. Write: Permissions, Wipf and Stock Publishers, 199 W. 8th Ave., Suite 3, Eugene, OR 97401.

Wipf & Stock
An Imprint of Wipf and Stock Publishers
199 W. 8th Ave., Suite 3
Eugene, OR 97401

www.wipfandstock.com

PAPERBACK ISBN: 979-8-3852-1268-2
HARDCOVER ISBN: 979-8-3852-1269-9
EBOOK ISBN: 979-8-3852-1270-5

02/27/24

The Scripture quotations contained in Scriptures and Reflections are from the *New Revised Standard Version Bible* (NRSV), copyright © 1989 by the Division of Christian Education of the National Council of the Churches of Christ in the U.S.A., and are used by permission. All rights reserved. The Psalm Responses are taken from *The Message: Catholic/Ecumenical Edition*. Copyright © 1993, 1994, 1995, 1996, 2000, 2001, 2002, 2013. Used by permission of NavPress Publishing Group.

His Mercy Endures Forever
Psalm 136:1

Give thanks to the LORD, / for he is good, for his mercy endures forever;

Give thanks to the God of praises, / for his mercy endures forever;

Give thanks to the guardian of Israel, / for his mercy endures forever;

Give thanks to him who formed all things, / for his mercy endures forever;

Give thanks to the redeemer of Israel, / for his mercy endures forever;

Give thanks to him who gathers the dispersed of Israel, / for his mercy endures forever;

Give thanks to him who rebuilt his city and his sanctuary, / for his mercy endures forever;

Give thanks to him who makes a horn to sprout for the house of David, / for his mercy endures forever;

Give thanks to him who has chosen the sons of Zadok to be priests, / for his mercy endures forever;

Give thanks to the shield of Abraham, / for his mercy endures forever;

Give thanks to the rock of Isaac, for his mercy endures forever;

Give thanks to the mighty one of Jacob, / for his mercy endures forever;

Give thanks to him who has chosen Zion, / for his mercy endures forever;

Give thanks to the King of the kings of kings, / for his mercy endures forever;

He has raised up a horn for his people, / praise for all his loyal ones.

For the children of Israel, the people close to him.

Praise the LORD!

—Sir 51:12

Psalm 136:1

Contents

Abbreviations	xi
Introduction	xv
Title: *His Mercy Endures Forever*	xv
His Mercy	xv
Endures Forever	xvi
Subtitle: *Biblical Reflections on Divine Mercy for Anytime*	xvi
Biblical Reflections	xvi
Divine Mercy	xvii
for Anytime	xvii
Using This Book	xvii
Notes on the Bible	xviii
Three Sections	xviii
Bibles	xx
Presuppositions	xxii
1 Hebrew Bible (Old Testament)	**1**
Torah	1
Grace	1
Mercy Seat	2
Mercy	3
History	4
No Mercy 1	4
Forgiveness	6
Prayer for Mercy 1	7
Wisdom Literature	8
Begging for Mercy	8
Cruel Mercy	9
No Mercy 2	10

vii

Contents

Mercy Obtained	11
Prophets	12
No Mercy 3	12
Show Mercy 1	13
No Mercy 4	14
Pilgrimage of Mercy	15
Favorable Mercy 1	17
Favorable Mercy 2	18
Merciless	19
Mercy Taken Away	20
Mercy on Ephraim	21
Restored by Mercy	22
Mercy Granted	23
Compassionate Face	25
Seek Mercy	26
Mercy for the Oppressed	28
Seeking Mercy	29
Mercy Belongs to God	30
In Mercy	32
Steadfast Love	33
Without Mercy	34
Remember Mercy	35
Withholding Mercy No More	36
Show Mercy	38
2 Apocrypha/Deuterocanonicals	40
Ways of Mercy	40
Grant Mercy	41
Mercy and Peace	43
Mercy and Safety	44
Finding Mercy	45
Great Mercy 1	47
Happiness and Mercy	48
Merciful Light	49
Mercy Showed 1	50
Mercy Showed 2	51
Turn for Mercy	52
Have Mercy	54
Mercy Again	55

Contents

Show no Mercy	57
Mercy Turned Again	58
Mercy Showed 3	59
Mercy on Inheritance	61
Grace and Mercy 1	62
Grace and Mercy 2	63
Pardoned in Mercy	65
Disciplined in Mercy	66
Expect Mercy	67
Healing Mercy	69
Wait for Mercy	70
Hope for Mercy 1	72
Majestic Mercy	73
Great Mercy 2	74
Mercy and Wrath	76
Great Mercy 3	77
Great Mercy 4	78
Great Mercy 5	79
Poured Mercy	81
No Mercy 5	82
Rejoice in Mercy	84
Welcomed Mercy	85
Mercy not Given Up	86
Prayer for Mercy 2	88
Hope for Mercy 2	89
Mercy and Righteousness	90
Mercy not Withdrawn	92
Find Mercy	93
Asking for Mercy 1	95
Mercy Endures Forever	97
Mercy for Mercy	99
Heaven's Mercy	100
God Shows Mercy	101
Hope for Mercy 3	103
Mercy as Discipline	105
Merciful Life	106
Time of Mercy	108
Show Mercy Soon	109

Pity and Mercy	111
Wrath Turned to Mercy	112
Beginning of Mercy	113
No Mercy 6	115
Angel of Mercy	116
Overtaken by Mercies	118
Governing with Mercy	119
Light of Mercy	121
Mercy Revealed	122
Asking for Mercy 2	124
Proclaim Mercy 1	126
Worthy of Mercy	127
Not Able to Have Mercy	129
Merciful	131
Mercy on Inheritance?	133
Set Free in Mercy	135
Merciful Afterlife	136
3 Christian Bible (New Testament)	138
Gospels	138
Mercy in Kind	138
Proclaim Mercy 2	140
Samaritan Mercy	141
Mercy not Available	143
Letters	144
Mercy: Divine Choice	144
Receive Mercy	146
Lexicon	149
Bibliography	151
Recent Books by Mark G. Boyer	153

Psalm 136:1

Abbreviations

BCE = Before the Common Era (same as BC = Before Christ)

CEV = The Contemporary English Version

CB (NT) = Christian Bible (New Testament)

Jas = Letter of James

John = John's Gospel

Jude = Letter of Jude

Luke = Luke's Gospel

Mark = Mark's Gospel

Matt = Matthew's Gospel

1 Pet = First Letter of Peter

Rev = Book of Revelation

Rom = Letter of Paul to the Romans

1 Thess = First Letter of Paul to the Thessalonians

CE = Common Era (same as AD = *Anno Domini*, in the year of the Lord)

HB (OT) = Hebrew Bible (Old Testament)

2 Chr = Second Book of Chronicles

Dan = Daniel

Deut = Deuteronomy

Abbreviations

Esth = Esther

Exod = Exodus

Ezek = Ezekiel

Gen = Genesis

Hab = Habakkuk

Hos = Hosea

Isa = Isaiah

Jer = Jeremiah

Job = Job

Josh = Joshua

1 Kgs = First Book of Kings

Lev = Leviticus

Mic = Micah

Neh = Nehemiah

Num = Numbers

Prov = Proverbs

Ps(s) = Psalm(s)

1 Sam = First Book of Samuel

2 Sam = Second Book of Samuel

Zech = Zechariah

NAB = *New American Bible Revised Edition*

NRSV = *New Revised Standard Version*

OT (A) = Old Testament (Apocrypha)

Add Esth = Additions to Esther

Bar = Baruch

2 Esd = Second Book of Esdras

Jdt = Judith

Abbreviations

1 Macc = First Book of Maccabees

2 Macc = Second Book of Maccabees

3 Macc = Third Book of Maccabees

Pr Man = Prayer of Manasseh

Sg. Three = Prayer of Azariah (Song of the Three Jews)

Sir = Sirach (Ecclesiasticus)

Tob = Tobit

Wis = Wisdom (of Solomon)

Peterson = *The Message*

/ = indicates where one line of poetic text ends and another begins

(biblical notation) = see the specific biblical verse(s) in parentheses for more information

– = range of verses following a colon (8:3–4)

— = range of verses from a verse in one chapter to a verse in another chapter (8:3—9:4)

a, b, c = designates first (a), second (b), third (c), etc. sentence in a verse of Scripture or a line of poetic text

His Mercy Endures Forever

Psalm 136:1

Introduction

Title: *His Mercy Endures Forever*

His Mercy

The source for the one hundred six entries on mercy in this book is the Bible: Hebrew Bible (Old Testament), Old Testament Apocrypha, and Christian Bible (New Testament). All the reflections provided in this book begin with biblical passages. The Scriptures have been selected from a variety of biblical material that mentions divine mercy; they are a representative biblical sample and are not exhaustive.

There is no single English word which adequately translates the Hebrew word *(c)hesed* or the Greek word *eleos*. Translators often use the English word *mercy*, but they also use forgiveness, generosity, pity, etc.; see the *Lexicon* at the end of this book for a list of English words and their meanings that are used to translate *(c)hesed* and *eleos*.

The *his* in *his mercy* refers, of course, to God. The phrase *his mercy endures forever* is found in the Old Testament Apocrypha book of Sirach 51:12; the complete hymn of thanksgiving that is inserted in the Hebrew Bible after 51:12 and before 51:13 can be found in the epigram on page v. The phrase can also be found in OT (A) The Prayer of Azariah and the Song of the Three Jews (1:67, 68 [Dan 3:89, 90]) and 1 Maccabees 4:24. In the Psalms, *(c)hesed* is often translated *steadfast love* (Pss 5:7; 6:4; 13:5; 17:7; 18:50; 21:7; 25:6, 7, 10; 26:3; 31:7, 16, 21; 32:10; 33:5, 18, 22; 36:5, 7, 10; 40:10, 11; 42:8; 44:26; 48:9; 52:8; 57:3, 10; 59:10, 16, 17; 61:7; 62:12; 63:3; 66:20; 69:13, 16; 77:8; 85:7, 10; 86:5, 13, 15; 88:11; 89:1, 2, 14, 24, 28, 33, 49; 90:14; 92:2; 94:18; 98:3; 107:1; 108:4; 109:21, 26; 115:1; 117:2; 118:1, 2, 3, 4, 29, 41, 64, 76, 88, 124, 149, 159; 130:7; 138:2, 8; 143:8, 12; 144:2;

Introduction

145:8; 147:11). Every verse of Psalm 136—twenty-six verses—contains the phrase *his steadfast love endures forever*. Steadfast love refers to God's firm and unwavering purpose, loyalty, and resolve when it comes to his intense feeling of tender affection and compassion for people. In the 1970 edition of *The New American Bible*, the verses of Psalm 136 state that *his mercy endures forever*.

Endures Forever

God's mercy or steadfast love lasts for all time. It is not like human infatuation that wears off after a while. God displays mercy constantly.

Subtitle: *Biblical Reflections on Divine Mercy for Anytime*

Biblical Reflections

Each of the one hundred six reflections begins with a biblical Scripture passage, which is followed by a reflection; the reflection gives background on the biblical selection and highlights its use of mercy. In some reflections, similar biblical uses are noted, and in some comparison translations from Bibles other than *The New Revised Standard Version* are given. The reflection is followed by a biblical psalm response, questions for meditating and/or journaling, and a prayer.

The biblical reflection is an exercise in spirituality, the method one chooses to nourish his or her spirit. The practices of spirituality are as varied as the people living on the earth. In this book, biblical passages with reflections, psalm responses, questions for meditation and/or journaling, and prayers are designed to nourish spirituality using some of the biblical references to God's mercy. In other words, the purpose of this book is to expose you—the reader—to the vastness of the mercy, compassion, tender love, and acceptance of the divine in the Bible. This author has written about spirituality extensively in other books; the reader can find a list of those at the back of this book.

Introduction

Divine Mercy

The phrase *Divine Mercy* refers to the love of God towards people. It often appears as *lovingkindness* in English translations. Divine mercy is expressed as benevolence, pity, piety, grace, and favor. For a non-exhaustive list of the meanings of mercy, see the *Lexicon* at the end of this book.

for Anytime

The entries in this book can be used to enhance one's spirituality anytime. In other words, this is not a book to be used only during a specific liturgical season (like Advent or Lent) or an annual season (like Spring or Winter). A person may read an entry and enhance his or her spirituality whenever he or she desires or whenever he or she deems it appropriate.

Using This Book

This book is designed to be used by individuals for private prayer. The goal of this book is to foster spirituality using biblical mercy that flows from the Bible. A six-part exercise is offered for all one hundred six entries.

1. **Title**: A short title is given to the entry. The title indicates a use of biblical mercy. Not only does the title give focus to the entry, but it imitates *Lectio Divina* (Divine Reading), the practice of reading a biblical passage and choosing a word or two from it for reflection, meditation, and prayer. The title is designed to promote mindfulness, the practice of maintaining a moment-by-moment awareness of thoughts, feelings, the body, and the surrounding environment. Mindfulness is the opposite of multitasking. Mindfulness is truly listening, fully tasting, deeply experiencing.

2. **Scripture**: Since the focus of the entry is found in the title, a verse or two from a Scripture passage—taken from the *New Revised Standard Version* of the Bible—illustrating the biblical source of the entry is provided.

3. **Reflection**: The Scripture passage is followed by a reflection on the biblical passage and its application to mercy. Throughout the reflections, the masculine pronoun for God, LORD, LORD God, etc. is used. The author understands that God is neither male nor female, but

to avoid the repetition of proper nouns repeatedly, he employs male pronouns, as they are also used in most biblical translations.

4. **Psalm Response**: A part of a biblical psalm—taken from *The Message*—is chosen to serve as a response to the reflection. Something in the psalm may spark prayer.

5. **Meditation/Journal**: The Psalm Response is followed by questions for personal meditation and/or journaling. The questions function as a guide for personal appropriation of the reflection, thus leading the reader into personal prayer and/or journaling. The meditation/journal questions are designed to foster a process of actively applying the reflection to one's life and further development of it; that is the spirituality dimension of the process. The question gets one started; where the meditation/journal goes cannot be predetermined. It may be a single statement or an idea with which one lingers for a few minutes, a few hours, or a few days. Such contemplation has no end; the reader decides when he or she has finished his or her exploration because he or she needs to attend to other things. People who like to journal—written or electronic—will find the questions appropriate for that activity.

6. **Prayer:** A prayer concludes the entry. The reader may use the prayer presented or compose his or her own in response to the spiritual awakening that has occurred for him or her.

Through this process of spirituality, the reader will come to a deeper knowledge of divine mercy and a closer relationship with God. Each person has experienced divine mercy, which to some degree shapes or forms his or her spirituality. In general, life is a sacred story authored by God and salted with divine mercy. Through the process of spirituality, people delve into the deeper meaning of their lives and discover where divine mercy has been revealed.

Notes on the Bible

Three Sections

The Bible is divided into two parts: The Hebrew Bible (Old Testament) and the Christian Bible (New Testament). The Hebrew Bible consists of thirty-nine named books accepted by Jews and Protestants as Holy Scripture. The

INTRODUCTION

Old Testament also contains those thirty-nine books plus seven to fifteen more named books or parts of books called the Apocrypha or the Deuterocanonical Books; the Old Testament is accepted by Catholics and several other Christian denominations as Holy Scripture. The Christian Bible, consisting of twenty-seven named books, is also called the New Testament; it is accepted by Christians as Holy Scripture. Thus, in this work:

—**Hebrew Bible (Old Testament)**, abbreviated **HB (OT)**, indicates that a book is found both in the Hebrew Bible and the Old Testament;

—**Old Testament (Apocrypha)**, abbreviated **OT (A)**, indicates that a book (or a part of a book) is found only in the Old Testament Apocrypha and not in the Hebrew Bible;

—and **Christian Bible (New Testament)**, abbreviated **CB (NT)**, indicates that a book is found only in the Christian Bible or New Testament.

In noting biblical texts, the first number refers to the chapter in the book, and the second number (following the colon) refers to the verse within the chapter. Thus, HB (OT) Isa 7:11 means that the quotation comes from Isaiah, chapter 7, verse 11. OT (A) Sir 39:30 means that the quotation comes from Sirach, chapter 39, verse 30. CB (NT) Mark 6:2 means that the quotation comes from Mark's Gospel, chapter 6, verse 2. When more than one sentence appears in a verse, the letters a, b, c, etc. indicate the sentence being referenced in the verse. Thus, HB (OT) 2 Kgs 1:6a means that the quotation comes from the Second Book of Kings, chapter 1, verse 6, sentence 1. Also, poetry, such as the Psalms and sections of Judith, Proverbs, and Isaiah, may be noted using the letters a, b, c, etc. to indicate the lines being used. Thus, Ps 16:4a refers to the first line of verse 4 of Psalm 16; there are two more lines of verse 4: b and c.

Because there may be a difference in the verse numbers between the *New Revised Standard Version* (NRSV) and the Vulgate (the Latin translation of the Septuagint, such as *The New American Bible Revised Edition* [NABRE]), alternative verse numbers appear in parentheses or brackets as necessary. This is true particularly with the Psalms, but with other books as well. Thus, NRSV Isaiah 9:2–7 is NABRE (Vulgate) Isaiah 9:1–6; NRSV Isaiah 9:2–4, 6–7 is NABRE (Vulgate) Isaiah 9:1–3, 5–6. Introductory material to Bibles usually indicates which verse-numbering is being used.

In the HB (OT) and the OT (A), the reader often sees LORD (note all capital letters). Because God's name (Yahweh or YHWH, referred to as the Tetragrammaton) is not to be pronounced, the name Adonai (meaning *Lord*) is substituted for Yahweh when a biblical text is read. When a biblical

Introduction

text is translated and printed, LORD (Gen 2:4) is used to alert the reader to what the text states: Yahweh. Furthermore, when the biblical author writes Lord Yahweh, printers present Lord GOD (note all capital letters for GOD; Gen 15:2) to avoid the printed ambiguity of LORD LORD. The Psalms in *The Message* substitute GOD (note all capital letters) for Yahweh. When the reference is to Jesus, the word printed is Lord (note capital L and lower-case letters; Luke 11:1). When writing about a lord (note all lower-case letters; Matt 18:25) with servants, no capital L is used.

In this book, *cf* (meaning *confer*) has not been used. Biblical notations placed in parentheses indicate where the reference can be found in the Bible. For example, the Second Book of Samuel records King David writing a song (2 Sam 22:1–51). The notation in parentheses is given to the reader, who may wish to look up the full reference in his or her Bible. In some instances, a number of notations appear in parentheses; again, the reader may wish to see the references in their contexts.

Bibles

Most Bible readers are not aware that there is no such thing as the original Bible! The fact is: There are Bibles. First, there is the Jewish Bible, often called the Hebrew Bible; its books were collected and completed between 70 and 90 CE based on the Jerusalem canon (collection) in this order: Torah (Genesis, Exodus, Leviticus, Numbers, Deuteronomy), Prophets (Isaiah, Jeremiah, Ezekiel, etc.), and Writings (Job, Psalms, Proverbs, etc). It is important to note the arrangement of the collected books. Second, there is—for want of a better name—the Christian Hebrew Bible or the Christian Old Testament, completed in the fourth century CE, but not defined until after the Reformation. It consists of Torah, Writings, and Prophets. It is important to note the (re)ordering of the collected books. Christianity took the Jewish (Hebrew) Bible and rearranged the order of its books into what is known among Christians as the Christian Hebrew Bible or the Christian Old Testament!

The Jerusalem canon, obviously, is the collection of biblical books used in Jerusalem and its environs. A large community of Jews, however, lived in Alexandria, Egypt. To the Jerusalem canon (books in Hebrew and Aramaic) they added books in Greek, the language they spoke; this collection is the Alexandrine canon. They also translated the Jerusalem canon's books from Hebrew and Aramaic into Greek. That translation, containing

Introduction

books and parts of books not in the Jerusalem canon, is called the Septuagint (abbreviated LXX). Later, the Septuagint was translated into Latin; it is known as the Vulgate. Every time a book of the Bible is translated, it picks up something and it loses something; that is because there is no such thing as literary equivalence.

Thus, we have (1) the Hebrew Bible—the Jewish Bible, (2) the Hebrew Bible (Old Testament)—the rearranged books of the Hebrew Bible, and (3) the Christian Bible—twenty-seven books originally written in Greek. The Protestant Bible contains only the books in the Jerusalem canon, but rearranged into the Old Testament, plus the Christian Bible books; the Catholic Bible contains the books in the Alexandrine collection plus the Christian Bible books.

The extra books or parts of books found in the Catholic Bible (and coming from the Alexandrine collection of the Jewish Bible), but not found in a Protestant Bible, are collectively referred to as the Apocrypha or Deuterocanonical Books. They include Tobit, Judith, additions to Esther, Wisdom (of Solomon), Sirach (Ecclesiasticus), Baruch, Letter of Jeremiah, Prayer of Azariah (addition to Daniel), Susanna (addition to Daniel), Bel and the Dragon (addition to Daniel), 1 Maccabees, 2 Maccabees, 1 Esdras, Prayer of Manasseh, Psalm 151, 3 Maccabees, 2 Esdras, and 4 Maccabees. Not every Christian group, such as Catholics, accepts all the books in the Apocrypha as Scripture; for example, out of the four books of Maccabees, Catholics accept only 1 and 2 Maccabees. In Catholic Bibles, the additional books are placed with similar books. Thus, First and Second Maccabees are inserted with the historical books; the books of Wisdom and Sirach are found in the wisdom literature section.

Thus, there is no single or original Bible; there are many Bibles; it depends on what books a specific denomination or group (Jews, Christians) accepts as Scripture. The Bible that contains any book that any group accepts as Scripture is *The Access Bible* (updated edition): *New Revised Standard Version with the Apocrypha*, general editors Gail R. O'Day and David Petersen, published in New York by Oxford University Press in 1999 and updated in 2011. *The Access Bible* presents the Old Testament books, the Apocryphal/Deuterocanonical Books, then the New Testament books. This book uses *The Access Bible* for all Scriptures and Reflections. This book also uses *The Message: Catholic/Ecumenical Edition, The Bible in Contemporary Language* by Eugene H. Peterson, published by ACTA Publications, Chicago, 2013, for all Psalm Responses.

Introduction

Thus, a Bible reader should keep in mind the following: In a Christian Bible, The Old Testament consists of the rearranged books found in the Hebrew (Jewish) Bible. Roman Catholics and some others add some books and parts of books to that Old Testament because they were found in the Alexandrine collection. In general, Protestants do not add books to the Old Testament; they follow the Jerusalem collection of books, but rearrange them as noted above. Almost all Christians accept the twenty-seven books of the New Testament; there are a few groups that reject one or another of the books in the collection.

Thus, as you can see, this can become difficult to navigate, especially when someone says, "The Bible says . . . ." The astute Bible reader needs to ask, "Which book in which Bible says that?" There is no such thing as the original Bible. There are Bibles, various libraries of books collected over three thousand years by individuals and groups who declared their collection (canon) to be Scripture.

Presuppositions

The HB (OT) begins as stories passed on by word of mouth from one person to another. Sometime during the oral transmission stage, authors decided to collect the oral stories and write them. A change occurs immediately. One does not tell a story the same way one writes a story. Repetition and correction occur in oral story-telling. Except for future emendations by copyists, single statements by characters and plot structure dominate written stories. Furthermore, in both oral and written story-telling, types or models are employed. In the HB (OT), for example, Joshua and Elijah are types of Moses. In the CB (NT) Elizabeth becomes a type of Hannah, who is herself a type of Sarah. When orally narrating or writing a story, the teller or author consciously creates one character as a type of another in order to make the character and his or her words and actions intelligible to the hearer or reader.

In the CB (NT) the oldest gospel is Mark's account of Jesus' victory. The author of Matthew's Gospel copied and shortened about eighty percent of Mark's material into his book and then added other stories to make the work longer. The author of Luke's Gospel copied and shortened about fifty percent of Mark's material into his orderly account and then added other stories to make the work much longer. The material shared by Matthew and Luke that is not found in Mark's Gospel is called Q—from the German

Introduction

word *Quelle*, meaning *Source*—by biblical scholars. Mark's Gospel begins as oral story-telling, lasting for about forty years in that form. An unidentified author, called Mark for the sake of convenience, collects the oral stories, sets a plot, and writes the first gospel around 70 CE. Because Jesus was expected to return soon, no one had thought about recording what he had said and done until Mark came along and realized that he was not returning as quickly as had been thought. About ten years after Mark finished his gospel, Matthew needed to adopt Mark's narrative—originally intended for a peasant Gentile readership—to a Jewish audience. And about twenty years after Mark finished his gospel, Luke needed to adapt Mark's poor Gentile-intended work for a rich, upper class, urban, Gentile readership. The author of John's Gospel did not know the existence of the other three works collectively named synoptic gospels.

Furthermore, gospels were not first intended to be read privately as is done today. They were meant to be heard in a group. The very low rate of literacy in the first century would have never dictated many copies of texts since most people could not read, and their standard practice was to listen to another read the stories to them. Thus, what began as oral story-telling passed on by word of mouth became written story-telling preserved in gospels. A careful reading of Mark's Gospel will reveal the orality still embedded in the text, especially evident in the repetition of words and the organization of stories in three parts. In rewriting Mark, Matthew and Luke remove the last traces of oral story-telling.

The letters of Paul are older than the gospels. Biblical scholars divide the letters of Paul into the authentic letters—those written by Paul (Romans, Galatians, Philippians, etc.)—and those written by someone else in Paul's name—second generation Pauline letters (Ephesians, Colossians, Titus, etc.). The latter group of letters usually develop Pauline thought for a new generation of Christians. The reader of letters needs to keep in mind that the letter was not addressed to him or her; it was addressed to a specific group of believers in the mid- to late-first century CE. In addition to the Pauline body of letters, there are other letters that were gathered and placed in the CB (NT) canon (collection), such as James, 1 and 2 Peter, Jude, etc. These anonymous letters were written in the name of an apostle to give them authority in the Christian communities to which they were addressed.

His Mercy Endures Forever
Psalm 136:1

1

Hebrew Bible (Old Testament)

Torah

Grace

Scripture: Israel said to his sons: "Take your brother [Benjamin] also, and be on your way again to the man; may God Almighty grant you mercy before the man, so that he may send back your other brother [Simeon] and Benjamin. As for me, if I am bereaved of my children, I am bereaved." (Gen 43:13–14)

Reflection: The above passage from the longer story about Joseph in the HB (OT) book of Genesis (37–50) occurs after the famine in the land of Canaan has intensified and after Jacob's (Israel's) sons already have made a trip to Egypt to procure provisions from their brother Joseph, whom they did not recognize. Also, they had left Simeon in Egypt, and they need to bring Benjamin with them on the second trip, according to Joseph, if they wanted to buy food a second time. Reluctantly, Jacob (Israel) concedes that they must go again to Egypt to buy grain, and that they need to bring Benjamin with them. Jacob (Israel) prays that El Shaddai, translated as God Almighty, will grant mercy to his sons before Joseph, even though he does not yet know that Joseph has become second in command to Pharaoh in Egypt.

This is one of the earliest uses of mercy in the HB (OT). The source of mercy, according to Jacob (Israel), who hopes to have his sons returned to him, is God. Peterson translates the Hebrew word as grace; thus Jacob's (Israel's) prayer is that the "Strong God give [the brothers] grace in [Joseph's] eyes." The CEV portrays Jacob (Israel) saying, "I pray that God All-Powerful will be good to you." The NAB, like the NRSV above, translates the Hebrew word as mercy. Jacob's (Israel's) prayer is that God will show generosity to the brothers through Joseph and send back Simeon and Benjamin to Jacob (Israel).

Psalm Response: "O my soul, bless GOD, / don't forget a single blessing! / He crowns you with love and mercy—a paradise crown. / He wraps you in goodness—beauty eternal. / He renews your youth—you're always young in his presence." (Ps 103:2, 4b–5)

Meditation/Journal: When has God showed you generosity (grace, mercy) through another person? Explain.

Prayer: Strong God, your generosity has no end. Out of your mercy wrap me in your blessings, and enable in me thanksgiving that renews my awareness of your presence today, tomorrow, and forever. Amen.

Mercy Seat

Scripture: "The LORD said to Moses: '... [Y]ou shall make a mercy seat of pure gold.... You shall make two cherubim of gold; you shall make them of hammered work, at the two ends of the mercy seat.... The cherubim shall spread out their wings above; overshadowing the mercy seat with their wings. They shall face one to another; the faces of the cherubim shall be turned toward the mercy seat. You shall put the mercy seat on the top of the ark; and in the ark you shall put the covenant that I shall give you." (Exod 25:1, 17a, 18, 20–21)

Reflection: While there are multiple mentions of mercy seat in the HB (OT) books of Exodus, Leviticus, and Numbers, it is in Exodus that the LORD tells Moses how to have it made. The NRSV translation presents a footnote for every time mercy seat is mentioned, indicating that it can also be translated as mercy cover. In other words, the top of the box containing the Torah (Law), the ark of the covenant, is where God sits when speaking with Moses. Peterson refers to this item as a lid or Atonement-Cover. CEV calls it the lid of the chest, and NAB refers to it as a cover, with a footnote explaining how the Hebrew word came to be translated as mercy seat or propitiatory.

The cherubim were half-animal (body of a lion or bull), half-human (head) creatures with wings thought to guard holy areas and kings by ancient peoples. Thus, the mercy seat, God's throne, or divine presence, is both a seat for the divinity, and it is guarded when the LORD, the king of Israel, speaks to his servant Moses. From his throne, God shows mercy to his people, that is, God forgives, excuses, releases his chosen people from inevitable punishment. God sits on the cover of the box containing the Torah (Law)—like a king on his throne—and forgives his people for not keeping the way of life he specified in the ark of the covenant!

Psalm Response: "Generous in love—God, give grace! / Huge in mercy—wipe out my bad record. / Scrub away my guilt, / soak out my sins in your laundry. / I know how bad I've been; / my sins are staring me down." (Ps 51:1–3)

Meditation/Journal: Recently, when has God released you from some inevitable punishment that contradicted the way of life to which he had called you? Explain.

Prayer: Your mercy, O LORD, far surpasses your justice. From your heavenly throne, use your mercy to wipe away my weaknesses and restore me to the life to which you call me to walk with you today, tomorrow, and forever. Amen.

Mercy

Scripture: "The LORD said to Moses: . . . 'I will make all my goodness pass before you, and will proclaim before you the name, "The LORD"; and I will be gracious to whom I will be gracious, and I will show mercy on whom I will show mercy.'" (Exod 33:17a, 19)

Reflection: After the Israelites have sinned by creating and worshiping the golden calf and the LORD declared them to be stiff-necked, Moses wants to be assured that God will continue to be with him and the people. In their dialogue—before the LORD instructs Moses to cut two new tablets of stone upon which God will write the Torah; the previous two were broken when Moses discovered the people worshiping the golden calf—the LORD tells

Moses that he will hide him in a cleft of the rock on Mount Sinai (Horeb) and cover him with his hand to protect Moses from God's glory and to keep Moses from seeing God's face.

According to the HB (OT) Exodus text, "The LORD passed before him, and proclaimed, 'The LORD, the LORD, / a God merciful and gracious, / slow to anger, / and abounding in steadfast love and faithfulness, / keeping steadfast love for the thousandth generation, / forgiving iniquity and transgression and sin . . .'" (Exod 34:6–7). In other words, God promises Moses that he will be gracious and he will show mercy, as he accompanies Moses and the Israelites to the Promised Land. Previously (Exod 20:5–6), the first element of God's character was punishment; in Exod 34:6–7, mercy, grace, love, faithfulness, and forgiveness trump the LORD's punishment. Peterson says that GOD declared himself to be a God of mercy and grace, endlessly patient. CEV has God declare that he is merciful, patient, loving, and trustworthy. NAB follows the NRSV above. God reveals to Moses his compassionate disposition, which flows from his generosity. God still requires a specific lifestyle from his chosen people, but he pardons their iniquity, their humanity, and renews his covenant with them.

Psalm Response: "GOD, my shepherd! / I don't need a thing. / Your beauty and love chase after me / every day of my life. / I'm back home in the house of GOD / for the rest of my life." (Ps 23:1, 6)

Meditation/Journal: When have you experienced God's goodness passing before you? Explain. When have you experienced God's mercy, grace, love, and forgiveness? How did you feel?

Prayer: LORD, LORD, you are a God merciful and gracious, abounding in steadfast love and faithfulness, and forgiving iniquity, transgression, and sin. Shine the glory of your face upon me and wrap me in your abundant mercy today, tomorrow, and forever. Amen.

History

No Mercy 1

Scripture: ". . . [I]t was the LORD's doing to harden [the] hearts [of the land's inhabitants] so that they would come against Israel in battle, in order that they might be utterly destroyed, and might receive no mercy, but be exterminated, just as the LORD had commanded Moses." (Josh 11:20)

Reflection: In the HB (OT), the LORD is often portrayed as hardening the hearts of the enemies of his chosen people. God tells Moses that he will harden Pharaoh's heart (Exod 4:21; 7:3; 9:12; 10:1, 20; 11:10; 14:4, 8). In biblical understanding, the heart is where human intellect and will intersect. The reader has no doubt that God's chosen people will enjoy the LORD's power. In the book of Joshua, God continues to harden the hearts of Israel's enemies, and they enjoy his power to conquer the land that was promised them. Thus, Israel's enemies receive no divine mercy. Their hostility and attacks are the LORD's doing, part of the divine plan to destroy them. Peterson avoids the hardening of heart concept and replaces it with God's idea; it was God's idea that Israel's enemies would stubbornly fight the chosen people. The CEV states that the LORD had told Moess that he wanted the people killed without mercy, while the NAB states that it was the LORD's doing to make Israel's enemies' hearts obstinate so that they might be put under the ban without mercy and destroyed, as God had instructed Moses.

While modern readers will struggle with the concept of a God who manipulates his people's enemies so that they are destroyed without mercy, ancient biblical authors had no battle with the idea. If the LORD created everything that existed, then he also controlled everything that existed. It is God's absolute control that is being presented in the hardening of hearts texts. According to the Bible, God chose a people (Hebrews, Israelites, Jews) and promised to give them the land of Canaan, which was already inhabited. Once the LORD got his people out of Egyptian slavery through Moses, he made the inhabitants of Canaan fight against Israel in battle, and he gave the Israelites the power to destroy them; the land's owners received no divine mercy; they were to be exterminated so that their land could be given to the Israelites, just as God had commanded Moses.

Psalm Response: "I look to you, heaven-dwelling God, / look up to you for help. / We're watching and waiting, holding our breath, / awaiting your word of mercy. / Mercy, GOD, mercy! / We've been kicked around long enough . . . ." (Ps 123:1, 2c–3)

Meditation/Journal: When have you experienced God answering your prayer, while simultaneously defeating your enemy without showing him/her/it mercy?

Prayer: All-powerful LORD God, you treat well whomever you want to treat well, and you are kind to whomever you want to be kind. While I petition you to shower your blessings upon me, please remember my enemies, persecutors, and abusers; pour upon them your gracious mercy that will guide them to confess your name today, tomorrow, and forever. Amen.

Forgiveness

Scripture: "... David said to [the prophet] Gad, 'I am in great distress; let us fall into the hand of the LORD, for his mercy is great; but let me not fall into human hands.'" (2 Sam 24:14)

Reflection: The biblical scene immediately before King David's words to the prophet Gad is the census the king orders. The census, the basis for conscription and taxation, is the result of the LORD's anger kindled against Israel (2 Sam 24:1). After getting the count, David realizes that he has sinned against God, who gives David three choices through the prophet Gad. David chooses to fall into the LORD's hand—three days of pestilence—because he trusts that his mercy will be great. God displays his great mercy by cancelling the pestilence early.

David's sin (2 Sam 24:10), distress (2 Sam 24:14), and the pestilence (2 Sam 24:15) are healed by God's great mercy. Similarly, in Mark's Gospel, Jesus heals a demoniac and sends him home to tell his friends about the mercy God has showed him (Mark 5:19). Likewise, blind Bartimaeus begs Jesus to have mercy on him (Mark 10:47), and he is healed. The author of Matthew's Gospel doubles not only the number of blind men (Matt 20:30) but also doubles the account (Matt 9:27) to highlight the divine mercy Jesus demonstrates. The author of Luke's Gospel presents a rich man seeking mercy from Abraham (Luke 16:24) and ten lepers seeking mercy from Jesus (Luke 17:13). In all cases, the bestowal of mercy results in healing.

Psalm Response: "Now answer me, GOD, because you love me; / Let me see your great mercy full-face. / Don't look the other way; your servant can't take it. / I'm in trouble. Answer right now!" (Ps 69:16–17)

Hebrew Bible (Old Testament)

Meditation/Journal: In what event of your life have you experienced God's great mercy of healing and forgiveness?

Prayer: Send me to my friends, O LORD, to proclaim your great mercy. Grant to me the divine mercy proclaimed by your Son, Jesus, today, tomorrow, and forever. Amen.

Prayer for Mercy 1

Scripture: Nehemiah prayed: "O LORD God of heaven, the great and awesome God who keeps covenant and steadfast love with those who love him and keep his commandments; O LORD, let your ear be attentive to the prayer of your servant, and to the prayer of your servants who delight in revering your name. Give success to your servant today, and grant him mercy in the sight of this man!'" (Neh 1:5, 11a)

Reflection: Nehemiah is the Persian King Artaxerxes' cupbearer. As such, he is responsible for ensuring the safety of the king's wine supply and often acting as the king's advisor. Around 445 BCE, Nehemiah, who was very concerned about Jerusalem, asked Artaxerxes to send him to the holy city to help rebuild it after it had been conquered by Nebuchadnezzar, King of Babylon, in 587 BCE. Artaxerxes grants his cupbearer's request and appoints him governor of Jerusalem. His mission is to rebuild the city's walls and the temple. In other words, the mercy Nehemiah requested that God show him through King Artaxerxes is given. CEV states that Nehemiah asked God to make him pleasing in Artaxerxes' sight. NAB states that Nehemiah asked God that he find favor in Artaxerxes' sight. According to Nehemiah, God's mercy—pleasure or favor—is displayed by the foreign King Artaxerxes. "... [T]he king granted me what I asked," writes Nehemiah, "for the gracious hand of my God was upon me" (Neh 2:8b). In other words, God was good to Nehemiah and favored him.

God works—displays mercy—through Nehemiah and through King Artaxerxes. God's work in Nehemiah is seen in his weeping for the Jews left in Jerusalem (Neh 1:3–4); those survivors, who escaped Babylonian captivity were living in a city whose walls were destroyed and whose gates were burned. It is also seen in Nehemiah's bold request of King Artaxerxes to release him from his cupbearer responsibilities and permit him to go to Judah. God's works—displays of mercy—through King Artaxerxes are seen in his granting of Nehemiah's request, his sending of letters with Nehemiah to guarantee safe passage, and a letter to the king's keeper of the forest to give him timber to make beams for the gates and walls of Jerusalem.

Psalm Response: "Show me how you work, GOD; / School me in your ways. / Take me by the hand; / Lead me down the path of truth. / You are my Savior, aren't you? / Mark the milestones of your mercy and love, GOD; / Rebuild the ancient landmarks!" (Ps 25:4–6)

Meditation/Journal: From whom have you received mercy or favor? In what specific way was God's hand upon you?

Prayer: O LORD God of heaven, you are the great and awesome God who keeps covenant and steadfast love with those who love you and keep your commandments. Let your ear be attentive and your eyes open to hear my prayer for mercy today, tomorrow, and forever. Amen.

Wisdom Literature

Begging for Mercy

Scripture: Job answered Bildad the Shuhite: "How . . . can I answer [God], / choosing my words with him? / Though I am innocent, I cannot answer him; / I must appeal for mercy to my accuser." (Job 9:14–15)

Reflection: After Bildad asks Job if God perverts biblical justice—upholding the innocent and punishing the guilty—Job replies that it is useless to enter litigation with God. Throughout the book named after him, Job maintains that he is innocent of any wrongdoing, but his accuser—God—cannot be summoned to court. Therefore, he tells Bildad that he must choose his words carefully and appeal to God for mercy. CEV and NAB state that all Job can do is beg for mercy from God, who is stronger than Job. In other words, God will not be summoned to court so that an accused person is found guilty or innocent. Job cannot contend with God and win; the only way open to him is to beg for mercy from God.

Because God is all-powerful and Job is not, later in the book he accuses God of causing his suffering by casting him into the hands of the wicked, breaking him, setting him like a target, and showing him no mercy (Job 16:11–13). That is why Job seeks God's pity. If God can feel sympathy or sadness because of Job's pain, Job hopes that the all-powerful God will regret the suffering he has imposed upon Job. Because God is responsible for everything that happens in the world, Job begs him to look upon Job's innocence and show him mercy.

Psalm Response: "Your mercies, GOD, run into the billions; / following your guidelines, revive me. / My antagonists are too many to count, / but I don't swerve from the directions you gave. / Take note of how I love what you tell me; / out of your life of love, prolong my life. / Your words all add up to the sum total: Truth. / Your righteous decisions are eternal." (Ps 119:156–157, 159–160)

Meditation/Journal: Recently, when have you felt guilty for something you did not do? To whom did you beg for mercy?

Prayer: LORD, I know that you can do all things, and no purpose of yours can be thwarted. Often, I utter what I do not understand, things too wonderful for me, which I do not know. My ears have heard your word, and my eyes have seen you in all you have made. I am but dust in your sight, and so I beg your merciful blessings today, tomorrow, and forever. Amen.

Cruel Mercy

Scripture: "The righteous know the needs of their animals, / but the mercy of the wicked is cruel." (Prov 12:10)

Reflection: A righteous person is one who knows what the right action to take is and does it. Thus, in the context of the proverb above, a righteous person is one who knows the needs of his animals—literally, his cattle—and he gives them food and water. Because "[t]he LORD does not let the righteous go hungry" (Prov 10:3)—God gives food and water to the righteous person—the righteous person gives food and water to his animals (cattle). While the righteous know what the right thing to do is and do it in imitation of God, who is righteous, the wicked show cruel mercy. The inner attitude of the wicked dictates that his animals (cattle) can fend for themselves. The wicked has no compassion and shows no kindness.

CEV states that good people are kind to their animals (cattle), but mean people are cruel, while NAB declares that the just take care of their livestock, but the compassion of the wicked is cruel. In other words, the righteous are aware of the needs of their animals (cattle) and prosper from the herd's good health, while the wicked will pay the price for their self-centeredness and cruelty. In a more contemporary context, the righteous are those who know the needs of their dog, but those who are ignorant dispense only mercy that is cruelty to the dog.

Psalm Response: "I can see now, GOD, that your decisions are right; / your testing has taught me what's true and right. / Oh, love me—and right now!—hold me tight! / just the way you promised. / Now comfort me so I can live, really live; / your revelation is the tune I dance to." (Ps 119:75–77)

Meditation/Journal: In what specific ways are you righteous? In what specific ways are you merciful? When has your mercy been cruel?

Prayer: The righteous are wise in your wisdom, O LORD, and they know the needs of their pets and they give them food, water, and medicine. Those who are not wise in your wisdom, God, are ignorant of their pets' needs and fail to give them food, water, and medicine. Grant me a generous amount of your mercy that I may share it with family and friends today, tomorrow, and forever. Amen.

No Mercy 2

Scripture: "The souls of the wicked desire evil; / their neighbors find no mercy in their eyes." (Prov 21:10)

Reflection: The proverb above declares that the spirit of the wicked prefers evil. That means that those who are mean consider only themselves in their selfishness. For example, mass murderers consider only the pleasure they receive from trapping and killing their victims. Corrupt rulers of countries are focused only on what they can get—money and power—by their harsh policies and war mongering. Those who constantly speed on highways are concerned only with how fast they can get to their destinations. Those who desire evil are so focused on doing wrong, according to the CEV, that they cannot see what they are doing to others; Peterson states that they love to make trouble at the level of mind, will, and how they live their lives. They must have whatever they have set their hearts upon, regardless of what trouble or sorrow it may cause to others. Desires need gratification for the wicked.

Anyone who has such a self-possessed neighbor knows that he or she receives no mercy. Even if the neighbor is a friend of the wicked, as states the CEV, nothing is felt for friends or neighbors, according to Peterson.

NAB declares that the wicked's neighbor gets no pity. No expression of sympathy, regret, or favor comes forth from those focused only on themselves. In other words, no love of neighbor is ever expressed or enacted. The selfish and hard-hearted are not capable of showing mercy to anyone.

Psalm Response: "I am innocent, LORD! / Won't you listen as I pray and beg for help? / I am honest! Please hear my prayer. / Don't let my brutal enemies / attack from all sides and kill me. / They refuse to show mercy, and they keep bragging." (Ps 17:1, 9–10)

Meditation/Journal: Whom do you know has a wicked (selfish) spirit? Does he or she show mercy (pity, compassion) to neighbors? Explain.

Prayer: O LORD, you taught your chosen people to love their neighbors as they love themselves. Your Son, Jesus, taught people that the love of neighbor as self represented one of two great commandments. Keep me from all evil desires, and inspire me to show mercy to my neighbors today, tomorrow, and forever. Amen.

Mercy Obtained

Scripture: "No one who conceals transgressions will prosper, / but one who confesses and forsakes them will obtain mercy." (Prov 28:13)

Reflection: Almost immediately after doing something wrong, people both young and old attempt to cover it, to pretend that whatever they did was not done. So, a child with crumbs on his or her chin will tell his or her parents that he or she had not put a hand in the cookie jar. Teenagers will declare forcefully that they did not engage in sex, even though the female is visibly pregnant. The adult manager of a restaurant will tell the owner that nothing happened to a disturbed customer. Those who conceal their transgressions do not prosper humanly because they are preoccupied with keeping their violation hidden. As everyone knows, it takes a lot of energy to conceal a wrong, and no energy is left to thrive.

    The author of the above proverb advocates owning the mistake and brining it to light to the proper person or authority in order to heal it. Modern psychology has taught nothing less. The transgression does not have to be brought into the open, but it does need to be revealed to those who have been hurt in some way. Repentance is required by the child with cookie crumbs on his or her chin so that a remedy can be found for the lie. Confession is required by sexually active and pregnant teenagers so that their parents can support them through their pregnancy. The restaurant manager needs to inform the owner about the disgruntled customer so that the owner knows what happened. Revealing transgressions brings them out of darkness and into light where mercy is obtained. Likewise, in our relationship with God; only the most foolish would think that they can hide their transgressions from the all-knowing LORD, who is ever ready to dispense mercy to those who confess and forsake their mistakes. Peterson states that one cannot whitewash offenses and get away with it; on the contrary, one finds mercy by admitting and leaving them.

Psalm Response: "Now GOD, don't hold out on me, / don't hold back your passion. / Your love and truth / are all that keeps me together. / When trouble ganged up on me, / a mob of sins past counting, / I was so swamped by guilt / I couldn't see my way clear. / More guilt in my heart than hair on my head, / so heavy the guilt that my heart gave out." (Ps 40:11–12)

Meditation/Journal: What wrong have you recently attempted to cover? What life did the cover-up rob from you? What wrong have you recently owned? What life did your confession give you? Who showed mercy to you?

Prayer: Nothing is hidden from your all-seeing eyes, LORD God. Give me the courage that comes from the Spirit to acknowledge my mistakes that I may experience your mercy today, tomorrow, and forever. Amen.

Prophets

No Mercy 3

Scripture: "[The Medes'] bows will slaughter the young men [of Babylon]; they will have no mercy on the fruit of the womb; their eyes will not pity children." (Isa 13:18)

Reflection: Chapter 13 of the book of the prophet Isaiah contains an oracle against Babylon. Basically, the oracle is a threat to that nation caught in world events that affected Israel and Judah. Isaiah declares that Babylon's oppressing power will be punished by God, who will incite the Medes against it. Because of the sufferings inflicted upon Judah by the Babylonians, the oracle contains a vengeful spirit.

Hebrew Bible (Old Testament)

The vengeful spirit is found in the Scripture verse above. Isaiah declares that the bows of the Medes will slaughter Babylon's young men; no Babylonian child will escape. The wrath of the LORD (Isa 13:13) will facilitate the Medes' actions of dashing infants to pieces, the plundering of homes, and the raping of women (Isa 13:16). Peterson says the Medes massacre the young, while CEV and NAB state that no pity is showed to babies and children. Thus, according to Isaiah, the God, who is rich in mercy, will show no mercy to the Babylonians, who took his chosen people into exile.

Psalm Response: "Give [my accusing judge, O God,] a short life, / and give his job to somebody else. / Make orphans of his children, / dress his wife in widow's weeds; / Turn his children into begging street urchins, / evicted from their homes—homeless. / May the bank foreclose and wipe him out, / and strangers, like vultures, pick him clean. / May there be no one around to help him out, / no one willing to give his orphans a break." (Ps 109:8–12)

Meditation/Journal: When have you asked God to take vengeance on your enemy? Explain. Why did you not want mercy to be showed to your enemy? In general, how do you feel about the LORD being wrathful or vengeful?

Prayer: I need your help, O LORD. Save me according to your steadfast love. With my lips I give you great thanks, and I praise you for standing by me in my need today, tomorrow, and forever. Amen.

Show Mercy 1

Scripture: "... [T]he LORD waits to be gracious to you, / therefore he will rise up to show mercy to you. / For the LORD is a God of justice; blessed are all those who wait for him." (Isa 30:18)

Reflection: In light of the fact that Judah has rejected the word of the Holy One of Israel (Isa 30:12), Isaiah, nevertheless, proclaims that the LORD is waiting to be gracious; indeed, he will arise to show mercy to his people in Jerusalem, which is under siege. Because the LORD is a God of justice, he does the right thing: he shows mercy to those who wait for him. In other words, those who display the ability to endure waiting or delay without becoming annoyed or upset are declared blessed, acceptable to God. One biblical example of this is found in the CB (NT) Gospel of Luke. Elizabeth and Zechariah were barren, but in their older years their waiting for God to show great mercy came to fruition, when Elizabth gave birth to John the Baptist (Luke 1:57–58, 72).

Peterson states that God is not finished; he is gathering strength to show mercy. He takes his time to do the right thing. With that assurance those who wait for him are lucky. CEV says that God, who always does the right thing, wants to show how kind he is and to have pity on his people. The prophet tells the inhabitants of Jerusalem that the LORD will hear their cry, answer their prayer, and be gracious to them. Their weeping will come to an end, when they receive God's gracious mercy. The author of the First Letter of Peter, likewise, declares that at one time mercy had not been received, but now mercy has been received (1 Pet 2:10).

Psalm Response: "Listen, GOD, I'm calling at the top of my lungs: / 'Be good to me! Answer me!' / When my heart whispered, 'Seek God,' / my whole being replied, 'I'm seeking him!' / Don't hide from me now." (Ps 26:7–9)

Meditation/Journal: When have you experienced God waiting to be gracious (to show mercy) to you? For what have you waited from God?

Prayer: Just God, you always do what is right for your people, who cry to you in prayer. Here I am awaiting your graciousness; arise and show me your mercy. As I await your justice, declare me blessed today, tomorrow, and forever. Amen.

No Mercy 4

Scripture: Thus says the LORD: "Sit in silence, and go into darkness, / daughter Chaldea! / For you shall no more be called / the mistress of kingdoms. / I was angry with my people, / I profaned my heritage; / I gave them into your hand, / you showed them no mercy; / on the aged you made your yoke / exceedingly heavy." (Isa 47:5–6)

Reflection: Chaldea, in the passage above, is another name for Babylon. The prophet Isaiah presents the LORD declaring that Babylon's power is at an end. In chapter 47, Babylon is presented as a mature young lady, who was "mistress of kingdoms," indicating that Babylon had absorbed many nations and plundered their lands and treasures. God indicates that he was angry with his chosen people; he gave them into Babylon's hand, but the powerful empire showed them no mercy, not even to the elderly (aged);

to lay a heavy yoke on the old is not acceptable behavior! Isaiah (God) is declaring that the presupposition that Babylon's power would remain unchecked forever is coming to an end. The LORD of hosts (Isa 47:4) has already chosen and anointed Cyrus, king of Persia, to overthrow Babylon (Isa 45:1–7).

Peterson portrays God stating that he turned over his people to Babylon, who had no compassion; instead, the empire put old men and women to cruel, hard labor. CEV states that the empire showed no mercy to the old, but was especially cruel. NAB uses the yoke metaphor, stating that it was a very heavy yoke that Babylon placed on the shoulders of the old. Through the prophet Isaiah, God promises to do to Babylon, through Cyrus, what Babylon did to the people of Judah; there is no one to save them (Isa 47:15d). In a similar vein, In the CB (NT) the Matthean Jesus indicts the scribes and Pharisees because they have neglected justice, mercy, and faith (Matt 23:23).

Psalm Response: ". . . God was fed up, his anger erupted—he cut down their brightest and best . . . . / When he cut them down, they came running for help; / they turned and pled for mercy. / They gave witness that God was their rock, / that High God was their redeemer, / But they didn't mean a word of it; / they lied through their teeth the whole time. / They could not have cared less about him, / wanted nothing to do with his Covenant. / And God? Compassionate! / Forgave the sin! Didn't destroy! / Over and over he reined in his anger, / restrained his considerable wrath." (Ps 78:31, 34–38)

Meditation/Journal: Do you think God can get angry with people? Explain. What mercy did God expect Babylon to show to the elderly? Why is showing mercy so important in biblical literature?

Prayer: Hear my plea for mercy, O LORD. Demonstrate your compassion by restraining your wrath, and bestow abundant blessings upon me. Fill me with your Holy Spirit that he may direct my steps in your way of life today, tomorrow, and forever. Amen.

Pilgrimage of Mercy

Scripture: "Seek the LORD while he may be found, / call upon him while he is near; / let the wicked forsake their way, / and the unrighteous their thoughts; / let them return to the LORD, that he may have mercy on them, / and to our God, for he will abundantly pardon." (Isa 55:6–7)

Reflection: Chapter 55 of the prophet Isaiah concludes the work of the prophet of the return of the Jews from Babylon to Jerusalem, otherwise known as Deutero-Isaiah. Biblical scholars isolate three prophets Isaiah (1:1—39:8; 40:1—55:13; and 56:1—66:24), each of whom wrote at a different time in history but were combined into one biblical book. While the opening line—"seek the LORD"—can mean to inquire or investigate, it is a term used biblically to indicate pilgrimage, the journey made to Jerusalem, where the LORD's Temple was located. The Jews returning from Babylonian captivity are exhorted to complete their journey to Jerusalem, where their God can be found. Among the returnees are the wicked and the unrighteous, who are told to return to God, who will have mercy on them and abundantly pardon their transgressions. What may appear as impossible—that the Jews would leave Babylon and return to Jerusalem—is possible for God. In the face of God, human beings can only appeal to his compassion and watch as God enacts what pilgrims think is impossible!

Peterson tells his readers to seek God while he is here to be found, and to pray to him, while he is close at hand. To be a true pilgrim, one must abandon one's previous way of thinking and turn to God, who is merciful and lavish with forgiveness. CEV states that God can still be found; he is near, merciful, and forgiving, and his thoughts are not like human thoughts. NAB declares that the God who is near is generous in merciful forgiveness. Therefore, there is no reason for the people to delay their pilgrimage to the holy city, where God awaits them.

Psalm Response: "Who can climb Mount GOD? / Who can scale the holy north-face? / Only the clean-handed, / only the pure-hearted; / Men who won't cheat, / women who won't seduce. / GOD is at their side; / with GOD's help they make it. / This, Jacob, is what happens / To God-seekers, God-questers." (Ps 24:3–6)

Meditation/Journal: What seemingly impossible thing has God done for you? Explain. What thinking about God have you recently abandoned? Why?

Prayer: I turn my thoughts to you, O LORD, because you are near and ready to find me. Forgive my unrighteousness and show me your abundant mercy. Fill my mind with your thoughts that my ways may be your ways today, tomorrow, and forever. Amen.

Hebrew Bible (Old Testament)

Favorable Mercy 1

Scripture: The LORD said: "Foreigners shall build up your walls, / and their kings shall minister to you; / for in my wrath I struck you down, / but in my favor I have had mercy on you." (Isa 60:10)

Reflection: These words from the prophet Isaiah are addressed to the Jews in Babylon. The expected return of the exiles to Jerusalem had not yet occurred, when Isaiah wrote the words above. Yes, a few had made the journey from Babylon to Jerusalem, but the return of a large group was still a dream (vision) when Isaiah wrote this passage. The City of the LORD, the Zion of the Holy One of Israel (Isa 60:14), had not yet been rebuilt. In order to facilitate the rebuilding of the city walls, God promises foreign help. God also declares that it was he who sent the Jews into Babylonian captivity, but they are back in his favor, and he is having mercy on them. God envisions a rebuilt city and Temple full of peace, righteousness, and prosperity. All he needs to do is to motivate his people—through the prophet Isaiah—to leave Babylon and return home.

CEV states that a new day is dawning. Jerusalem's walls will be rebuilt. God admits that he punished his people in his anger, but he has decided to be kind and merciful. Peterson shouts at Jerusalem to get out of bed. God hit hard, but now he displays tenderness. NAB says that God struck hard, but in his good will he shows mercy. In his letter to the Philippians, Paul declares that God has showed mercy to his co-worker Epaphroditus, who was ill and nearly died. In showing mercy to Epaphroditus, God has also showed mercy to Paul, who is sending his co-worker to the Philippians (2:25–30).

Psalm Response: "GOD, my God, I yelled for help / and you put me together. / GOD, you pulled me out of the grave, / gave me another chance at life / when I was down-and-out. / All you saints! Sing your hearts out to GOD! / Thank him to his face! / He gets angry once in a while, but across / a lifetime there is only love. / The nights of crying your eyes out / give way to days of laughter." (Ps 30:2–5)

Meditation/Journal: When have you received favorable mercy from God? What foreign help did you receive? Explain.

Prayer: My God, I thank you for all the times you have showed me favorable mercy. Throughout my life continue to be gracious to me, that I may praise you today, tomorrow, and forever. Amen.

Favorable Mercy 2

Scripture: "I will recount the gracious deeds of the LORD, / the praiseworthy acts of the LORD, / because of all that the LORD has done for us, / and the great favor to the house of Israel / that he has shown them according to his mercy, / according to the abundance of his steadfast love." (Isa 63:7)

Reflection: Chapter 63 of the prophet Isaiah, from which comes the above verse, portrays God enacting a day of vengeance on those who had enslaved his people. He is acting decisively out of love for his chosen people. Suddenly, the narrator (Isaiah) breaks into the LORD's words with his memories of God's gracious and praiseworthy deeds of the past which favored Israel, his people. The LORD's presence saved them in the past; his love and pity redeemed them; he lifted them and carried them in past days through his servant, Moses (Isa 63:9, 11–14). In other words, he displayed his favorable mercy, which flowed from his steadfast love.

CEV proclaims the LORD's kind deeds and the kindness and goodness he showed to the people of Israel. Peterson portrays the narrator making a list of God's gracious dealings, his generous bounties, his great goodness, his lavish compassion, and his extravagant love. NAB lauds the LORD's loving deeds, glorious acts, and immense goodness. In the CB (NT) the author of Luke's Gospel presents Zechariah, the father of John the Baptist, declaring that the Lord God of Israel "has looked favorably on his people and redeemed them" (Luke 1:68). ". . . [H]e has shown the mercy promised to [Jewish] ancestors, / and he has remembered his holy covenant . . ." (Luke 1:72). In other words, God's favorable mercy, lavish grace, and steadfast love do not waver for the people he chose to be his own.

Psalm Response: ". . . [H]ow blessed all those in whom you live [, GOD,] / whose lives become roads you travel . . . . / All sunshine and sovereign is GOD, / generous in gifts and glory. / He doesn't scrimp with his traveling companions. / It's smooth sailing all the way with GOD-of-the-Angel-Armies." (Ps 84:5, 11–12)

Meditation/Journal: What gracious, merciful, and loving deeds has God done in your life? Make a list.

Prayer: Look upon me, O LORD. You are my Father, my Redeemer from of old. Turn toward me, your servant, and enact gracious, merciful, and loving deeds, like you did in past ages. Hear my prayer today, tomorrow, and forever. Amen.

Merciless

Scripture: "Thus says the LORD: / See, a people is coming from the land of the north, / a great nation is stirring from the farthest parts of the earth. / They grasp the bow and the javelin, / they are cruel and have no mercy, / their sound is like the roaring sea; / they ride on horses, / equipped like a warrior for battle, / against you, O daughter Zion!" (Jer 6:22–23)

Reflection: In 597 BCE, Nebuchadnezzar invaded Jerusalem and Judah and deported King Jehoiachin to Babylon. In the king's place, Nebuchadnezzar installed Zedekiah, as a client king. However, in 587 Judah revolted and Nebuchadnezzar returned and mercilessly destroyed Jerusalem, its walls, and the Temple. The prophet Jeremiah repeatedly warned Judah's kings that the great nation coming from the north (Babylon) was going to attack and conquer the small kingdom of Judah. Nebuchadnezzar's warriors were coming, according to Jeremiah, and they were equipped with bows and javelins. Jeremiah describes them as coming against daughter Zion (Jerusalem); they are cruel and merciless. There are so many of them on horseback that they sound like the sea's roar. These are the cavalrymen leading the way for the infantrymen.

CEV emphasizes the Babylonians' preparation for war with merciless, well-armed troops mounted on galloping horses, ready to attack Jerusalem. NAB declares the army pitiless, as does Peterson, who adds that they are armed to the teeth and vicious, tramp, tramp, tramping, riding hard on war horses in battle formation. From history we know that Jeremiah's words were not heeded. Nebuchadnezzar's war machine captured Jerusalem and Zedekiah, who, before his eyes were burned with hot irons, watched his three sons be slaughtered. Then, he was taken to Babylon, where, with Jehoiachin, he died, and the line of King David came to an end!

Psalm Response: "And now, watch this! People pouring / out of the north, hordes of people, / A mob of kings stirred up / from far-off places. / Flourishing deadly weapons, / barbarians they are, cruel and pitiless. / Roaring and relentless, like ocean breakers, / they come riding fierce stallions. / In battle formation, ready to fight . . . ." (Jer 50:41–42)

Meditation/Journal: Recently, whose words, which came true, did you not heed? What got in the way of your listening? What mercilessness did you experience?

Prayer: O LORD, through your prophet Jeremiah, you warned your chosen people about the cruel and merciless warriors—armed with bow and javelin on horseback—coming from the north. Send people to me to announce your warnings, and open my ears that I may hear and heed them today, tomorrow, and forever. Amen.

Mercy Taken Away

Scripture: ". . . [T]hus says the LORD: Do not enter the house of mourning, or go to lament, or bemoan them; for I have taken away my peace from this people, says the LORD, my steadfast love and mercy." (Jer 16:5)

Reflection: The Scripture passage above comes from the sixteenth chapter of the prophet Jeremiah in which several voices debate the meaning of the impending exile of Judah to Babylon. The first nine verses are the voice of God, who tells Jeremiah not to find a wife and not to beget children (Jer 16:1–4). He is not to attend funerals, either. His abstentions create a breach in the social network of the community. In other words, Jeremiah is to stand alone, isolated from his Jewish community. His life is to be a sign of what is about to happen: exile. Life as he and the Jerusalem community have known it is coming to an end; there are to be no marriages, no children, no formal funerals. The LORD makes clear to Jeremiah that he has removed peace, steadfast love, and mercy from his people.

CEV states that Jeremiah is forbidden to visit the family of a deceased member or to show any sorrow since God no longer loves, blesses, or shows pity to his people. NAB records that God has withdrawn compassion from his people. Peterson presents God declaring that he has quit caring about what happens to his people. All of these are hard words to read or hear. It is a terrible thing to hear the LORD state that he is withdrawing his peace, love, and mercy from his chosen people and delivering them to exile, captivity, and death.

Psalm Response: "Watch this: God's eye is on those who respect him, / the ones who are looking for his love. / He's ready to come to their rescue in bad times; / in lean times he keeps body and soul together. / We're depending on GOD; / he's everything we need." (Ps 33:18–20)

Meditation/Journal: When have you experienced mercy being taken away from you? Explain. When have you stood alone, isolated from your community? Explain. Do you find God's words about withdrawing his peace, love, and mercy from his chosen people hard to hear? Explain.

Prayer: LORD God, you were known for you peace, steadfast love, and compassion by your chosen people. When your prophet Jeremiah announces that you are withdrawing those, I become ill. Give your peace to me; renew your steadfast love in me; and show pity to me, as you did in past ages. Guide my steps in your ways today, tomorrow, and forever. Amen.

Mercy on Ephraim

Scripture: "Is Ephraim my dear son? / Is he the child I delight in? / As often as I speak against him, / I still remember him. / Therefore I am deeply moved for him; / I will surely have mercy on him, says the LORD." (Jer 31:20)

Reflection: After the death of King Solomon, the single kingdom he ruled split into the Northern Kingdom of Israel and the Southern Kingdom of Judah. Israel was defeated by the Assyrians in 722 BCE. At the time of Jeremiah (627–587) there was a hope that both Israel and Judah would be reunited into one nation; this hope is expressed in chapters 30 and 31 of the prophet Jeremiah. In the passage above, the LORD poses two questions to himself: Is Israel—referred to as Ephraim—my dear son? Is Israel my darling child? Those rhetorical questions are followed by the LORD's emotional reflection. His profound and overwhelming words indicate that every time he speaks or thinks of Israel, he is overpowered, and he cannot help but show him compassion. In other words, God has sympathy for the suffering Israel endured at the hands of the Assyrians. This prompts him to inspire Jeremiah to write: "The days are surely coming, says the LORD, when I will make a new covenant with the house of Israel and the house of Judah" (Jer 31:31).

Peterson captures the emotion of the verse by referring to Israel as the child in whom God takes pleasure; at the mention of Israel's name, God's heart bursts with longing for him. Softly and tenderly he waits for Israel. CEV states that God loves Israel best of all. Ephraim, according to the NAB, is God's favored son; God's heart stirs for him so much that the LORD must show him compassion. The pain felt by Jeremiah because the ten northern tribes had been conquered and carried off, leaving the land devastated, is embodied in the image of a matriarch (Rachel) lamenting and bitterly weeping for her children, who are no more (Jer 31:15).

Psalm Response: "As parents feel for their children, / GOD feels for those who fear him. / He knows us inside and out, / keeps in mind that we're made of mud. / Men and women don't live very long; / like wildflowers they spring up and blossom, / But a storm snuffs them out just as quickly, / leaving nothing to show they were here. / GOD's love, though, is ever and always, / eternally present to all who fear him . . . ." (Ps 103:13–17)

Meditation/Journal: What words would you use to capture God's emotion in the Scripture passage above? What does the emotion expressed in the Scripture passage above imply about God's mercy?

Prayer: Out of all the people on the earth, you chose the Israelites to be your own, O LORD. In the fullness of time, through your son, Jesus, you chose all people to be your own. With your grace give me the vision to see and understand your emotional and merciful compassion expressed by your prophet Jeremiah and live it today, tomorrow, and forever. Amen.

Restored by Mercy

Scripture: "Thus says the LORD: Only if I had not established my covenant with day and night and the ordinances of heaven and earth, would I reject the offspring of Jacob and of my servant David and not choose any of his descendants as rulers over the offspring of Aberaham, Isaac, and Jacob. For I will restore their fortunes, and will have mercy upon them." (Jer 33:25–26)

Reflection: Immediately before the LORD sent Jeremiah to King Zedekiah of Judah to tell him that God was giving Jerusalem to the king of Babylon

(Jer 34:1–5), chapter 33 narrates the restored relationship between the people and God that the LORD promises! (Jer 33:14) God promises to restore the kingship and the priesthood and to reunite the peoples of Israel and Judah. Some were saying that the LORD had rejected both Israel and Judah; they were no longer regarded as a nation (Jer 33:23–24). God assures his prophet that his covenant with day and night was in working order, and sky and earth were functioning the way he set them going. He did not disown Jacob's descendants nor David's descendants established to rule the descendants of Abraham, Isaac, and Jacob—both the Northern and the Southern kingdoms. He promises to restore their fortunes by having mercy on them.

As Peterson states, God's covenant with day and night, with sky and earth are functioning the way they were created to work. If they were not working the way God made them, then, and only then, could Jeremiah think that God had disowned the descendants of Abraham and David. CEV states that God will never break his agreement with day and night or let the sky and earth stop obeying his commands; in the same way he would never reject the descendants of Abraham or break his promise about having a Davidic descendant as ruler of Judah. God promises kindness and success to his people. According to NAB, after Nebuchadnezzar destroys Jerusalem and the kingship, God will restore his people's fortunes and show them mercy.

Psalm Response: "Thank GOD-of-the-Angel-Armies. He's so good! His love never quits." (Jer 33:11b)

Meditation/Journal: What experience of restoration after some type of destruction have you experienced? What role did God play in your restoration? What mercy did God show you?

Prayer: Following destruction you bring restoration, O LORD. After years in captivity, you brought back your people to Judah and Jerusalem and enabled them to flourish in your sight. When I am broken, in your mercy send the Holy Spirit to fill me with new life. I praise you today, tomorrow, and forever. Amen.

Mercy Granted

Scripture: Jeremiah said: "Thus says the LORD the God of Israel, to whom you sent me to present your plea before him: If you will only remain in this land, and I will build you up and not pull you down; I will plant you, and not pluck you up; for I am sorry for the disaster that I have brought upon you. Do not be afraid of the king of Babylon, as you have been; do not be afraid of him, says the LORD, for I am with you, to save you and to rescue you from his hand. I will grant you mercy, and he will have mercy on you and restore you to your native soil." (Jer 42:9–12)

Reflection: The passage above is a part of chapters 37 through 44 of the prophet Jeremiah, most likely written by Baruch, Jeremiah's scribe; 37:1—44:30 narrates the last months of the prophet's life in Jerusalem. The subsection, 40:7—41:18, centers on Johanan, a military officer and an associate of Gedaliah, the governor of Judah appointed by King Nebuchadnezzar of Babylon after he captured and destroyed Jerusalem. After Gedaliah is killed, Johanan and his commanders approach Jeremiah and ask him whether they should stay in Judah or migrate to Egypt. Jeremiah agrees, and ten days later has an answer: The LORD desires that they remain in Judah, where he will save, rescue, and show them mercy. The narrative (Jer 42:13–21) explains what will happen if they, nevertheless, decide to go to Egypt. Johanan and his forces accuse Jeremiah of lying (Jer 43:2). Johanan leads the survivors, along with Jeremiah and Baruch, to Egypt, not obeying the voice of the LORD (Jer 43:4–10).

Underlying the above passage is the presupposition that the LORD is the supreme ruler of the world. God set Nebuchadnezzar over the world (Jer 27:6); the LORD controls the king's hand and exercises his mercy through the king. Jeremiah has made it clear that any nation that will not submit to Nebuchadnezzar's yoke and serve him will perish (Jer 27:8–11). Because God is in control of all world events, those people remaining in Judah should not fear the king of Babylon. The all-powerful God, who apologizes for the disaster he has brought upon Jerusalem (Jer 43:10c), promises to rescue the remnant of Judah from Nebuchadnezzar's hand, pour mercy upon the remnant (Peterson), show pity (NAB), protect (CEV), and restore the people to their native soil.

Psalm Response: "Alongside Babylon's rivers / we sat on the banks; we cried and cried, / remembering the good old days in Zion. / Alongside the quaking aspens / we stacked our unplayed harps . . . . Oh, how could we ever sing GOD's song / in this wasteland? / If I ever forget you, Jerusalem, / let my fingers wither and fall off like leaves. / Let my tongue swell and turn

Hebrew Bible (Old Testament)

black / if I fail to remember you, / If I fail, O dear Jerusalem, / to honor you as my greatest." (Ps 137:1–2, 4–6)

Meditation/Journal: What do you think about God's apology ("I am sorry for the disaster that I have brought upon you" [Jer 43:10])? Do you think God is the supreme ruler of the world? Explain.

Prayer: LORD, my God, you build up, plant, and protect what you have created. Grant me the grace to be aware of your presence with me, to save me, and to rescue me. Let me know your abundant mercy today, tomorrow, and forever. Amen.

Compassionate Face

Scripture: ". . . [T[hus says the Lord GOD: Now I will restore the fortunes of Jacob, and have mercy on the whole house of Israel; and I will be jealous for my holy name. Then they shall know that I am the LORD their God because I sent them into exile among the nations, and then gathered them into their own land. I will leave none of them behind." (Ezek 39:25–28)

Reflection: A weary reader may get tired of reading texts about the Babylonian exile of the people of Judah. After all, the exile is treated in the prophet Isaiah, in the prophet Jeremiah, and in the prophet Ezekiel. Ezekiel went into Babylonian exile with the Jews. The above passage begins with God declaring that he will restore Jacob's fortunes; change is about to begin, because the LORD is going to show his merciful face to the whole house of Israel. His zeal for doing this is to reveal his holy name to the people who profaned it. In other words, the tribulation of the exiles, the dishonoring of God's name, will soon lie in the past. An alternate reading of verse 26 declares that the people will bear (not forget) their shame. God's mercy is not a summons to blind forgetfulness; the people must bear their guilt for their treachery. Then, Israel's God, the LORD, who led the people away among the nations, will bring them back to their own land. God promises never to hide his merciful face from them. Indeed, he is going to seal the deal by outpouring his divine spirit, who will engender the final irrevocable union of the LORD with his people.

CEV states that God will restore Israel and show the people that he, their God, is holy. The people will remember their evil and how they disgraced their God and be ashamed. Foreign nations will see the LORD bringing back his people to their own land. His spirit will live in them. NAB states that God pities Israel. The nations will become aware that Judah went into exile because the people betrayed him, and because of their betrayal, he hid his face. Now, zealous for his holy name, he will show his face to his people and pour his spirit upon them. Peterson states that God has compassion on the people he sent into exile. After pouring his spirit upon them, he'll use them to display his holiness to the nations. In the CB (NT), the author of Luke's Gospel portrays Mary, the mother of Jesus, declaring that the Mighty One has helped Israel, his servant, in remembrance of his mercy, according to his promise to her ancestors (Luke 1:54).

Psalm Response: "Light, space, zest— / that's GOD! / So, with him on my side I'm fearless, / afraid of no one and nothing. / God holds me head and shoulders / above all who try to pull me down. / I'm headed for his place to offer anthems / that will raise the roof! / Already I'm singing God-songs; / I'm making music to GOD. / Listen, GOD, I'm calling at the top of my lungs: 'Be good to me! Answer me!' / When my heart whispered, 'Seek God,' / my whole being replied, / 'I'm seeking him!' / Don't hide from me now!" (Ps 27:1, 6–9)

Meditation/Journal: When have you seen God's face? Explain. What do you consider God's holy name to be? Explain. How is God's spirit alive in you?

Prayer: LORD, you are my light and my salvation. Your compassionate face I seek; do not hide your merciful face from me. Grant that I may live in your presence all the days of my life and behold your beauty today, tomorrow, and forever. Amen.

Seek Mercy

Scripture: ". . . Daniel went to his home and informed his companions, Hananiah, Mishael, and Azariah, and told them to seek mercy from the God of heaven concerning this mystery, so that Daniel and his companions with the rest of the wise men of Babylon might not perish." (Dan 2:17–18)

Reflection: The HB (OT) book of the prophet Daniel opens with tales that establish Daniel's credibility as a righteous Jew in Babylonian exile. Nebuchadnezzar, king of Babylon, ordered four, young Jewish males to his court to be trained for service in his empire. After having a bad dream, he summoned his court magicians, enchanters, and sorcerers (Dan 2:2) to tell him his dream and to interpret it for him, but none could be found who could do what he asked. Daniel volunteered to reveal to the king his dream and interpret it in time. Then Daniel went home to inform his three companions what was going to take place. He told them to seek mercy from God concerning the mystery of the king's dream and to give him the wisdom to narrate the dream to the king and interpret it for him. In contrast to Babylonian wisdom, the four young men pray for mercy! According to the tale, God answered their prayer and revealed the mystery of Nebuchadnezzar's dream in a vision of the night; Daniel does not have a dream; he is given a vision by the God of heaven. The mercy that is sought from the God of heaven is divine wisdom, which will make Daniel a supremely competent interpreter throughout the book.

While NAB states that Daniel asked his companions to implore the mercy of God regarding the mystery of Nebuchadnezzar's dream, both CEV and Peterson state that he told them to pray that God would be merciful in solving the mystery of the dream and explaining its meaning. In Babylon, dream interpretation was widely practiced, especially by the royalty of the kingdom. Daniel's ability comes from God, and, thus, his wisdom trumps that of the king who destroyed Daniel's land and brought him in captivity (exile) to Babylon. Thus, even in exile God helps his people!

Psalm Response: "Blessed be the name of God, / forever and ever. / He knows all, does all: / He changes the seasons and guides history, / He raises up kings and also brings them down, / he provides both intelligence and discernment, / He opens up the depths, tells secrets, / sees in the dark—light spills out of him! / God of all my ancestors, all thanks! all praise! / You made me wise and strong. / And now you've shown us what we asked for. / You've solved the king's mystery." (Dan 2:19–23)

Meditation/Journal: When have you recently sought God's mercy in prayer to understand something? What vision did you receive? How did God help you? Explain.

Prayer: From age to age your name, O God, is blessed. I join the unending chorus in praising you for the insight, knowledge, and understanding you have bestowed upon me, and I seek your mercy and inspiration today, tomorrow, and forever. Amen.

Mercy for the Oppressed

Scripture: Daniel said to King Nebuchadnezzar: "... O king, ... it is a decree of the Most High that has come upon my lord the king: ... [S]even times shall pass over you, until you have learned that the Most High has sovereignty over the kingdom of mortals and gives it to whom he will. Therefore, O king, may my counsel be acceptable to you: atone for your sins with righteousness, and your iniquities with mercy to the oppressed, so that your prosperity may be prolonged." (Dan 4:24–25, 27)

Reflection: King Nebuchadnezzar's building program was well known in the ancient world. After the king of Babylon narrates a dream to Daniel about a cosmic tree reaching from the earth to the heavens with beautiful foliage and abundant fruit with animals living under it and birds nesting in its branches, Daniel tells him that the tree was he. Nebuchadnezzar had conquered most of the then-known world and built it into an empire. Because the king had not yet learned that it was the Most High God who had given him greatness, Daniel told him that for seven years—a number signifying the divine—he would be insane, until he learned that God was sovereign and any sovereignty he enjoyed was delegated to him by the Most High. Once he learned that and repented of his sins and iniquities by showing mercy—in imitation of God—to the oppressed—the Jews in Babylonian captivity—reason would be restored to him.

This Danielic tale is not history. It contains the element of the arrogant king—the cosmic tree—who is about to be cut down. However, unlike other such tales, the king repents. Thus, this story (Dan 4:1–37) narrates a stubborn hope for the repentance and conversion of the most arrogant of tyrants (Gentile powers) and for recognition of the Most High God. Peterson presents Daniel telling the king to take his advice, break with his sins, and start living for others by looking after the needs of the down-and-out. CEV advises the king to have mercy on the mistreated, while NAB advises kindness to the poor. If the king repents (and he does), he will have a good life.

Psalm Response: "[The High God's] sovereign rule lasts and lasts, / his kingdom never declines or falls. / Life on this earth doesn't add up to much, / But God's heavenly army keeps everything going. / No one can interrupt his work, / no one can call his rule into question. Everything he does is right, / and he does it the right way. / He knows how to turn a proud person / into a humble man or woman." (Dan 4:34–35, 37)

Meditation/Journal: What of your actions demonstrate that the Most High God has sovereignty over the earth? What of your actions do not demonstrate that the Most High God has sovereignty over the earth? In what specific ways do you show mercy to the oppressed (the down-and-out, the mistreated)? In what specific ways has God prolonged your prosperity (given you a good life)?

Prayer: Most High God, you live forever! Your sovereignty is everlasting, and your kingdom endures from one generation to the next. Fill me with your truth and justice, and motivate me to show mercy to the oppressed. Make my life prosperous in compassion today, tomorrow, and forever. Amen.

Seeking Mercy

Scripture: "The conspirators came and found Daniel praying and seeking mercy before his God. Then they approached the king and said concerning the interdict, 'O king! Did you not sign an interdict, that anyone who prays to anyone, divine or human, within thirty days except to you, O king, shall be thrown into a den of lions?' The king answered, 'The thing stands fast, according to the law of the Medes and Persians, which cannot be revoked.' Then they responded to the king, 'Daniel, one of the exiles from Judah, pays no attention to you, O king, or to the interdict you have signed, but he is saying his prayers three times a day.'" (Dan 6:11–13)

Reflection: The tale about Daniel in the lions' den is set during the time of Darius I (522–486 BCE), who organized the Persian Empire into twenty administrative districts. Over all of them, he intended to appoint Daniel (Dan 6:3). The administrators, who didn't want an exiled Jew to have power second only to the king over them, conspired to have the king issue an interdict that forbade anyone in the empire from praying to anyone, divine or human, for thirty days, except to the king; the punishment for doing so was to be thrown into a den of lions. According to the story, Daniel—an exiled Jew—who knew about the interdict, continued to go to his house, face Jerusalem, kneel, and three times a day pray to his God. The spying conspirators see what he is doing—seeking mercy before his God—and report to King Darius what they have seen. They insist that the legislated punishment be given, and even though the king tries to save Daniel, he cannot revoke the rule he has made. Thus, Daniel is tossed into the lions' den. However, God sends an angel to shut the lions' mouths, and Daniel is not harmed. In response, the king orders that the conspirators, their wives, and their children be thrown into the lions' den (Dan 6:19–26).

The purpose of the narrative (6:1–28) is to demonstrate how God protects righteous Jews from foreign monarchs, who either demand worship of other gods or worship of themselves. Daniel's faithfulness to God—praying three times a day—not only demonstrates his religiosity, but it becomes the source for his being thrown into the lions' den and the reason for his rescue from the hungry beasts. King Darius is presented as a victim of the plot of the conspirators. He calls upon Daniel's God to save his faithful servant (Dan 6:18), and he establishes the kingdom of God (Dan 6:26). NAB states that Daniel was pleading for help from his God, while both Peterson and CEV declare that he was asking God for help. He was seeking the magnanimity and generosity of God.

Psalm Response: "King Darius published this proclamation to every race, color, and creed on earth: 'Peace to you! Abundant peace! / I decree that Daniel's God shall be worshiped and feared in all parts of my kingdom. / He is the living God, world without end. His kingdom never falls. / His rule continues eternally. / He is a savior and a rescuer. / He performs astonishing miracles in heaven and on earth. / He saved Daniel from the power of the lions.'" (Dan 6:26–27)

Meditation/Journal: When have you sought mercy (magnanimity, generosity) from God? What did you face? How did God help you? Explain.

Prayer: In the morning, at noon, and in the evening, I seek your mercy, O LORD, and you hear my voice. Come to my help and redeem me from whatever I face. You, who are enthroned from of old, hear and answer me today, tomorrow, and forever. Amen.

Mercy Belongs to God

Scripture: "Ah, Lord, great and awesome God, keeping covenant and steadfast love with those who love you and keep your commandments, we have sinned and done wrong, acted wickedly and rebelled, turning aside from your commandments and ordinances. To the Lord our God belong mercy and forgiveness, for we have rebelled against him, and have not obeyed the voice of the LORD our God by following his laws, which he set before us by his servants the prophets." (Dan 9:4b–5, 9–10)

Reflection: Chapter 9 of the book of Daniel presents the prophet examining the writings of Jeremiah, particularly the passages dealing with the length of the Babylonian exile (Jer 25:11, 12; 29:10): seventy years (Dan 9:2). In order to understand, Daniel turns to the Lord God to seek an answer by prayer and supplication with fasting, sackcloth, and ashes (Dan 9:3). Daniel's prayer, a part of which forms the above passage, follows; the lengthy prayer occupies more than half of the chapter. Daniel's awareness that according to Jeremiah the exile would last seventy years distresses him. That is why he confesses his people's sin and requests God's mercy. In the HB (OT) book of Exodus, God had revealed himself as the LORD, a merciful and gracious God (Exod 34:6). "We do not present our supplication before you on the ground of our righteousness," prays Daniel, "but on the ground of your great mercies" (Dan 9:18c). Daniel ends his prayer asking God to listen and act for his own sake (Dan 9:19b).

NAB records that Daniel recalls that God shows mercy toward those who love him and keep his commandments and precepts, and that he is just in all he does. CEV echoes NRSV above about God being merciful and forgiving. Peterson records Daniel praying that God's compassion is the people's only hope; the people, according to Daniel, do not deserve a hearing from God.

Psalm Response: "Master, listen to us! / Master, forgive us! / Master, look at us and do something! / Master, don't put us off! / Your city [Jerusalem] and your people [Israel] are named after you: /You have a stake in us!" (Dan 9:19)

Meditation/Journal: For what have you prayed based on God's great mercies? When has God's compassion been your only hope? Explain.

Prayer: Listen to the prayer of your servant, O LORD, and let your face shine upon him (her). I do not present my need out of my own righteousness, but on my hope for your great mercies. Hear me, O LORD; listen, forgive, and act today, tomorrow, and forever. Amen.

In Mercy

Scripture: "On that day, says the LORD, you will call me 'My husband,' and no longer will you call me, 'My Baal.' And I will take you for my wife forever; I will take you for my wife in righteousness and in justice, in steadfast love, and in mercy. I will take you for my wife in faithfulness; and you shall know the LORD." (Hos 2:16, 19–20)

Reflection: The prophet Hosea is concerned about the Northern Kingdom of Israel's loyalty to God. He denounces Israel's worship of the Canaanite god Baal, and he uses the metaphor of marriage to illustrate Israel's relationship with God. God is described as a faithful husband, while Israel is described as his faithless wife. Hosea addresses the Northern Kingdom of Israel before its fall to Assyria in 721 BCE. On the day of salvation, God promises to remove the names of the Baals from his people's lips and enter a new and perpetual covenant with his wife (Israel), because it is the right and just action to take in everlasting love and in compassion. The LORD displays a loving sensitivity founded on an indissoluble togetherness; this intimate relationship begins with God's alluring Israel into the wilderness and speaking tenderly to her (Hos 2:14). Such a new experience in the desert will make his wife respond to him, like she did when she was led out of the land of Egypt (Hos 2:15). By showing mercy to Israel, God desires a new relationship of salvation.

CEV enlarges the marriage metaphor by portraying God substituting justice, fairness, love, kindness, and faithfulness for a bride price, the customary money paid to the parents of the bride by the intended husband. NAB enlarges the marriage metaphor by portraying God betrothing Israel to him forever with justice, judgment, loyalty, compassion, and fidelity. And Peterson presents God telling his bride that he is going to wash out of her mouth with soap all the false-god names and then marry her forever in a true and proper way in love and tenderness; he will never leave her nor let her go.

Psalm Response: "All you who fear GOD, how blessed are you! / how happily you walk on his smooth straight road! / You worked hard and deserve all you've got coming. / Enjoy the blessing! Revel in the goodness! / Stand in awe of God's Yes. / Oh, how he blesses the one who fears GOD! (Ps 128:1–2, 4)

Meditation/Journal: What metaphor(s) do you use to illustrate your relationship with God? What role does divine mercy play?

Hebrew Bible (Old Testament)

Prayer: As I walk in your ways, O LORD, make me happy, like a husband and wife find delight in each other. Know me in righteousness, justice, steadfast love, and mercy today, tomorrow, and forever. Amen.

Steadfast Love

Scripture: "Let us know, let us press on to know the LORD.... For I desire steadfast love and not sacrifice, the knowledge of God rather than burnt offerings." (Hos 6:3a, 6)

Reflection: The astute reader will immediately notice that the word *mercy* does not appear in the Scripture text above. However, the author of Matthew's Gospel interprets steadfast love as mercy: "I desire mercy, not sacrifice" (Matt 9:13; 12:7), the Matthean Jesus tells the Pharisees. The prophet Hosea presents the LORD stating what is acceptable to him, and it is not what had been presumed for ages: burnt offerings. He desires loyalty, as stated by NAB, and faithfulness, as stated by CEV. Also, he desires that his people have knowledge of God. He, the efficacious God of Israel, enters into relationship with his people. To know him is to experience him and live with him in a communion of trust and obedience. He is not satisfied with burnt offerings, because they may indicate only pious rituals. Indeed, Psalm 51 states that he takes no delight in sacrifice and is not pleased with burnt offerings (Ps 51:16). "The sacrifice acceptable to God is a broken spirit; / a broken and contrite heart, O God, you will not despise" (Ps 51:17). Mercy (steadfast love, loyalty, faithfulness) is genuine worship from the heart, and it reveals God's relationship to his people.

That is the point the Matthean Jesus makes when quoting Hosea's words. Jesus is eating with tax collectors and sinners—a nice, English word for prostitutes—something a good Jew should not do! That is why he tells the Pharisees to learn the meaning of mercy, generosity showed to an offender. Without mercy, sacrifice is meaningless. Likewise, after Jesus' disciples walk through a field on the sabbath and pluck heads of grain to eat, the Pharisees remind him that such action is unlawful on the sabbath. When people are hungry, mercy trumps the sabbath law. Divine mercy is greater than the law (Torah) states Jesus. Peterson captures the spirit of the verse, presenting God declaring that he is after love that lasts, no more religion. God states that he wants his people to know him, not to go to more prayer meetings. In other words, enacted mercy is prayer.

Psalm Response: "My head is high, GOD, held high; / I'm looking to you, GOD; / No hangdog skulking for me. / I've thrown in my lot with you; / You won't embarrass me, will you? / Or let my enemies get the best of me? / Show me how you work, GOD; / School me in your ways. / Take me by the hand; / Lead me down the path of truth. / You are my Savior, aren't you? / Mark the milestones of your mercy and love, GOD . . . . (Ps 25:1–3a, 4–6a)

Meditation/Journal: In what specific ways do you demonstrate steadfast love (mercy, loyalty, faithfulness) to God? When have you advocated for law instead of mercy? Explain.

Prayer: I am striving to know you and your ways, O LORD. With your Spirit help me to recognize where I can give steadfast love and enact mercy as a prayer acceptable to you. Grant my petition today, tomorrow, and forever. Amen.

Without Mercy

Scripture: O LORD, "You have made people like the fish of the sea, / like crawling things that have no ruler. / The enemy brings all of them up with a hook; / he drags them in his seine; / so he rejoices and exults. / Therefore he sacrifices to his net / and makes offerings to his seine; / for by them his portion is lavish, / and his food is rich. / Is he then to keep on emptying his net / and destroying nations without mercy?" (Hab 1:14–17)

Reflection: The typical military machine at the time of King Nebuchadnezzar of Babylon (605–562 BCE) was built from horse-drawn chariots and cavalry. However, it is not a military metaphor that the prophet Habakkuk uses in his prayer, but a fishing metaphor. According to Habakkuk, the people of the world are like fish in the sea; they are caught by the Babylonian hook, drug out with the Babylonian net, and trapped in the Babylonian seine. Habakkuk goes so far as to state that the Babylonians worship their nets and seine, because those provide the fisherman (Nebuchadnezzar) with much rich food. Then, the prophet asks the LORD a question: Is Nebuchadnezzar going to be allowed to continue fishing, that is, destroying nations without mercy?

While Habakkuk is primarily concerned about God's just rule over a world—Nebuchadnezzar's empire—that appears to him to be overwhelming unjust, his fishing metaphor aptly captures Babylon's greatest king's military campaigns and construction projects. As the longest-reigning king of the Chaldean dynasty, Nebuchadnezzar was one of the most powerful rulers of the then-known world. As a warrior-king, he conquered the Assyrian empire (which had conquered the northern kingdom of Israel). He destroyed the southern kingdom of Judah and its capital city, Jerusalem. Jeremiah thinks of him as a cruel enemy, but the prophets understand him to be God's instrument to punish his people's disobedience. Habakkuk's fishing metaphor refers to Nebuchadnezzar's lavish building projects in Babylon and the fine dining he enjoyed. What bothered Habakkuk the most was that the great warrior and builder king did everything without showing mercy to the fish (nations) he caught.

Psalm Response: "Be good to me, God—and now! / I've run to you for dear life. / I'm hiding out under your wings / until the hurricane blows over. / I call out to High God, / the God who holds me together. / God delivers generous love, / he makes good on his word." (Ps 57:1–2, 3b)

Meditation/Journal: What metaphor could you use to describe the empire you have built? How did you show mercy to those you conquered?

Prayer: LORD God, I keep my eyes on you until you show me your abundant mercy. When I am alone, I need your help; do not let me be caught in the nets of those seeking their own gain, and give me the vision to show mercy to those who have been snared by others. Keep watch over all today, tomorrow, and forever. Amen.

Remember Mercy

Scripture: "O LORD, I have heard of your renown, / and I stand in awe, O LORD, of your work. / In our own time revive it; / in our own time make it known; / in wrath may you remember mercy." (Hab 3:2)

Reflection: The three-chapter HB (OT) book of the prophet Habakkuk ends with a hymn (psalm) that begins with a petitionary introduction (Hab 3:2) and then narrates a theophany (Hab 3:3–15) before ending with a conclusion (Hab 3:16–19). The prophet acknowledges that he has heard about God from his ancestors, and based on the rumors he is awestruck—down on his knees, according to Peterson—and stopped in his tracks. He acknowledges that the LORD has a reputation, which he prays will be revived during his lifetime. Presuming that God is angry with his people and letting the Babylonians conquer them, he asks the LORD to remember the mercy he showed in the past and to do for him what God once did for his ancestors, namely, to deliver him and them from his enemies. In NAB he seeks compassion, while in CEV he seeks mercy. Habakkuk does not think that God is capable of forgetting; he urges him to release his wrath and remember and display his mercy (compassion) again.

The theophany, the manifestation of God, that follows describes God's march into battle and conquest of his enemies to save his people (Hab 3:13). Typical of biblical theophanies is the LORD's brightness, like the sun (Hab 3:4), earthquake (Hab 3:6–7), and the force of chaos—water (Hab 3:8–15). In the conclusion (Hab 3:16–19), despite the lack of food, the prophet rejoices in God, who gives him strength and saves him. Just like the LORD conquers all cosmic forces, so does he conquer Israel's historical enemies!

Psalm Response: "GOD's on his way again, / retracing the old salvation route . . . . / Skies are blazing with his splendor, / his praises sounding through the earth, / His cloud-brightness like dawn, exploding, spreading, / forked-lightning shooting from his hand— / what power hidden in that fist! / He stops. He shakes Earth. / He looks around. Nations tremble. / The age-old mountains fall to pieces; / ancient hills collapse like a spent balloon. / The paths God takes are older / than the oldest mountains and hills. / You [, GOD,] were out to save your people, / to save your specially chosen people." (Hab 3:3a, 4, 6, 13a)

Meditation/Journal: In your times of wrath (anger), when have you remembered mercy (compassion)? Make a list, and explain how God's mercy was manifested to you through the ways you showed mercy to others.

Prayer: I have read about your presence to people in the past, O LORD, and I am awed by the degree of compassion you have showed. Grant that in my own time I may experience your mercy and presence today, tomorrow, and forever. Amen.

Withholding Mercy No More

Scripture: ". . . [T]he angel of the LORD said, 'O LORD of hosts, how long will you withhold mercy from Jerusalem and the cities of Judah, with which you have been angry these seventy years?' . . . [T]he angel who talked with

Hebrew Bible (Old Testament)

me said to me, Proclaim this message: Thus says the LORD of hosts; I am very jealous for Jerusalem and for Zion." (Zech 1:12, 14)

Reflection: The passage above is the first of eight visions in the prophet Zechariah. The angel of the LORD, the action of God delivering a message to people, thinks out loud and asks himself how much longer will he withhold mercy from the cities of Judah (including Jerusalem). The angel mentions that God has been angry for seventy years; however, the Babylonian captivity, which came to an end after fifty years (587–538 BCE), is over when Zechariah is writing his book (520–519 BCE). Zechariah portrays the LORD declaring, "... I have returned to Jerusalem with compassion; my house shall be built in it..." (Zech 1:16). Those are gracious and comforting words, including his jealousy for Jerusalem and for Zion, a hill in the city where David placed the ark of the covenant in a tent before Solomon built the first Temple. According to Peterson, God is very possessive of Jerusalem and Zion. In CEV, God is very protective of Jerusalem and Zion, and he promises them pity.

Zechariah's words to the returnees are full of hope; God oversees history, and he plans to restore the fortunes of Judah. Those who left Babylon and traveled to Jerusalem found ruins—broken walls of the city and a destroyed Temple. Needless to say, the future did not look bright; in fact it looked like a lot of hard work! That is why Zechariah attempts to instill hope and to urge people to begin the process of rebuilding their city, its Temple, and their institutions during this post-exilic period. God's mercy will be withheld no longer. His former angry words have become words of grace, comfort, and compassion.

Psalm Response: "Generous in love—God, give grace! / Huge in mercy—wipe out my bad record. / Make Zion the place you delight in, / repair Jerusalem's broken-down walls. / Then you'll get real worship from us, / acts of worship small and large...." (Ps 51:1, 18–19)

Meditation/Journal: What gracious and comforting words have you heard from the LORD? Have you ever experienced God's jealousy? Explain.

Prayer: After fifty years of Babylonian captivity, you raised up King Cyrus of Persia to defeat the Babylonians and let your people return to Jerusalem and Judah, O LORD. You spoke gracious and comforting words to them, giving them hope for their rebuilt future. When I feel hopeless, share your grace and mercy with me. Hear my prayer today, tomorrow, and forever. Amen.

Show Mercy

Scripture: "The word of the LORD came to Zechariah, saying: Thus says the LORD of hosts: Render true judgments, show kindness and mercy to one another, do not oppress the widow, the orphan, the alien, or the poor; and do not devise evil in your hearts against one another." (Zech 7:8–10)

Reflection: After presenting eight visions, the prophet Zechariah focuses on creating a just society in which true judgments are made, kindness and mercy are showed, and those most vulnerable—the widow, orphan, alien, and poor—are not oppressed. According to Zechariah, religious rituals are meaningless apart from the practice of justice in all areas of life. That was the message delivered by prophets before Zechariah, but the Jews would not listen to them. Zechariah uses the example of his ancestors' behavior to teach a lesson to the Babylonian exiles who have returned to Jerusalem. NAB urges the returnees to show kindness and compassion to one another, as does Peterson.

Zechariah's words are echoed in Matthew's Gospel; Jesus tells the crowd on the mountain, "Blessed are the merciful, for they will receive mercy" (Matt 5:7), and it is illustrated in the parable about the king who forgave a slave's debt, but the slave would not forgive his fellow slave's debt. The king asks him, "I forgave you all that debt because you pleaded with me. Should you not have had mercy on your fellow slave, as I had mercy on you?" (Matt 18:32–33) In the parable, the slave does not answer the king's question. The reader must answer it: Yes, I should have mercy on my fellow slave, just as the king had mercy on me! In Luke's Gospel, Jesus illustrates the one human being showing mercy to another human being by telling the story about a Jew falling into the hands of robbers; he was showed pity by a Samaritan—a person detested by Jews. After narrating the parable about a priest and Levite passing by the Jew in the ditch, the Lukan Jesus asks his listeners, "Which of these three, do you think, was a neighbor to the man who fell into the hands of the robbers?" (Luke 10:36) A lawyer answers, "The one who showed him mercy" (Luke 10:37). Jesus tells him to go and imitate the Samaritan! He is sent to show kindness and mercy to other human beings, no matter their ethnic origin.

Psalm Response: "Sing hymns to God; / all heaven, sing out; / clear the way for the coming of Cloud-Rider. / Enjoy GOD, / cheer when you see him! / Father of orphans, / champion of widows, / is God in his holy house. / God makes homes for the homeless, / leads prisoners to freedom, / but leaves rebels to rot in hell." (Ps 68:4–6)

Meditation/Journal: In what specific ways have you showed mercy to others? How do the ways you have showed mercy to others reflect the mercy God has showed to you?

Prayer: Through your prophet Zechariah, you teach me to show kindness and mercy to others, O LORD. Make me deeply aware of those in need of kindness and mercy, and give me the strength to remove oppression from widows, orphans, aliens, and the poor. Blessed be your holy name today, tomorrow, and forever. Amen.

Psalm 136:1

2

Apocrypha/Deuterocanonicals

Ways of Mercy

Scripture: "... [W]ith much grief and anguish of heart I [, Tobit,] wept, and with groaning began to pray: 'You are righteous, O Lord, / and all your deeds are just; / all your ways are mercy and truth; / you judge the world.'" (Tob 3:1–2)

Reflection: The OT (A) book of Tobit is a novella set at the time of the fall of the northern kingdom of Israel to Assyria. Tobit, who has walked in the ways of truth and righteousness (Tob 1:3), has been exiled to Nineveh (Tob 1:3), where he continues to practice his Jewish piety. After sending his son, Tobias, to look for a poor person to share his dinner, Tobias returns to tell him about a murdered Jew, whose body Tobit retrieves and buries. Then, Tobit sits in his courtyard and falls asleep. Sparrow droppings fall onto his face and blind him. Meanwhile his wife, Anna, earns money by doing women's work—weaving fabric (Tob 2:11). One of her buyers gave her a young goat, but Tobit did not believe her, and told her to return it to its owners. Anna reproves her blind husband, who has not been able to perform charitable or righteous deeds because of his blindness. This puts Tobit in a state of grief and anguish of heart. Groaning, he begins to pray.

    First, he acknowledges that God is just; he does the right thing because it is the right thing to do. Second, God lives the way of mercy and truth (or peace, according to Peterson and NAB). What Tobit is acknowledging is that the way God lives is a lifestyle of compassion and truth (or peace). Tobit has been imitating the judge of the world's lifestyle by showing mercy: going to Jerusalem for the festivals, bringing the first fruits and firstlings of the flock and tithes to Jerusalem (Tob 1:6–8). He buried the dead and fed the poor (Tob 1:16–18). After four years of blindness, he begins his prayer in grief and anguish, and he asks God to take his life (Tob 3:6). God, however, has a plan, which is revealed by reading the rest of the novella.

Psalm Response: "You're just, O Lord. All your works are just. All your ways demonstrate mercy and truth. You're the judge of the world; take up my case and rule leniently. Don't take the rod to me for the sins and negligence of me and my forebears that were committed right under your very nose. We didn't obey the letter of your Law, so you handed us over to pillagers and plunderers. You kicked us out of the land you promised our ancestors, landing us where we knew nobody. You made us a joke to the Gentiles. Now your judgments are upon us, many and true, wringing from me and my people the precise amount of punishment our sins deserved; you wouldn't have had to do that if we'd acted properly and walked justly in your presence." (Tob 3:2–5)

Meditation/Journal: What divine ways of mercy have you experienced in your lifetime?

Prayer: Blessed are you, ever-merciful God, and blessed be your name forever. Your ways of mercy are numerous. Fill me with your grace that raises my awareness of compassion and tenderness you have bestowed upon others through me. All praise be to you today, tomorrow, and forever. Amen.

Grant Mercy

Scripture: Raphael said to Tobias: "Now when you are about to go to bed with [Sarah], both of you must first stand up and pray, imploring the Lord of heaven that mercy and safety may be granted to you. Do not be afraid, for she was set apart for you before the world was made. You will save her, and she will go with you." (Tob 6:18b–d)

Reflection: As the novella Tobit unfolds, more characters are introduced. First, there is Sarah, Tobias' kinswoman through his father's (Tobit's) lineage. She prays to God, asking him to take her life; she has been married to seven husbands, and each one dies on their wedding night! Second, there is Raphael (otherwise known as Azariah), sent by God to heal Tobit's blindness, to see to the marriage of Tobias, Tobit's son, and Sarah, and to accompany Tobias on a trip to collect money Tobit left in trust in Media. On the way to Media, Raphael instructs Tobias what to do with the parts of a fish Tobias catches in the Tigris River; the gall, heart, and liver can be used as medicine. The gall can be used to heal Tobias' blindness, and the heart and liver can be used to drive away the demon that kills Sarah's husbands on their wedding night!

Raphael's instructions to Tobias are to burn the fish's heart and liver on coals, and with Sarah to pray to the Lord for mercy and safety (health, according to Peterson; protection, according to NAB) on their wedding night. Raphael assures Tobias that he will save Sarah, who has been set apart for him from before the world was created by God, and she will join him as his wife, when they return to his father and mother. Sarah's parents are Raguel and Edna; after Raphael and Tobias find their home, they are invited to dine with them. Tobias requests Sarah's hand in marriage from Raguel, who, based on previous experiences, is reluctant to give her to him. After Tobias insists, Raguel grants his request, but while the couple are on their way to bed, Raguel instructs his servants to dig a grave for Tobias, only to discover the next morning that both are still alive! Raguel is not confident that the Lord will grant mercy to the newly-married couple! However, Raphael (Azariah) and Tobias are!

Psalm Response: "Blessed are you, God of our fathers [and mothers]! Blessed be your name forever and ever! May the heavens and all your creatures bless you from age to age! You made Adam and gave him Eve. From both came the human race. You said, did you not, that it was not good for man to be alone? That he needed a helper, a look-alike? And so you provided [and granted mercy]." (Tob 8:5b–6)

Meditation/Journal: What of your prayers to God for mercy have been granted? Make a list.

Prayer: God of my ancestors, you are blessed by everyone and everything you have created. Hear my prayer and grant mercy to (name), and grant mercy to me all the days of my life. Amen.

Mercy and Peace

Scripture: Raguel said: "'[Sarah] is given to you [, Tobias,] in accordance with the decree in the book of Moses, and it has been decreed from heaven that she be given to you. Take your kinswoman; from now on you are her brother and she is your sister. She is given to you from today and forever. May the Lord of heaven, my child, guide and prosper you both this night and grant you mercy and peace.' Then Raguel summoned his daughter Sarah. When she came to him, he took her by the hand and gave her to Tobias, saying, 'Take her to be your wife in accordance with the law and decrees written in the book of Moses. Take her and bring her safely to your father. And may the God of heaven prosper your journey with his peace.'" (Tob 7:11e–12)

Reflection: Raguel's prayer that the Lord of heaven grant mercy and peace to Tobias and Sarah is, first, a petition that Tobias not die on his wedding night, like Sarah's previous seven husbands, and, second, a petition, that the contracting of marriage between Tobias and Sarah will result in a long, peaceful life together. Raguel, whose name means *friend of God*, refers to the couple as brother and sister, common terms for spouses. He also hopes that the Lord of heaven will serve as their guide, leading them in the right direction. Here it is important to note that Raguel does not know that Azariah is Raphael, meaning *God heals*, who has already given Tobias the proper procedure to follow on his wedding night to save himself from the demon that has killed Sarah's previous seven husbands. In other words, God is healing Sarah.

Raguel also expresses his hope that the Lord of heaven will make the couple thrive or flourish, and that he will make successful their journey to Tobias' home. After offering such good wishes to Tobias and Sarah, Raguel prepares a marriage contract in order to follow the law of Moses. The law of Moses is known as the levirate marriage law, which states that if a husband died and left no heirs, the nearest male relative was to marry the widow to produce heirs for the deceased. After seven previous husbands, Tobias is next in line to marry Sarah. After they have eaten the marriage supper,

Edna, Raguel's wife, prepares the bridal chamber. She tells her daughter to take courage—to be brave— and she hopes that the Lord of heaven will grant her joy on her wedding night.

Psalm Response: "Blessed are you, God of our fathers [and mothers]! Blessed be your name forever and ever! May the heavens and all your creatures bless you from age to age! [In mercy and peace] I take this woman, my cousin, as my lawful wedded wife, not to quiet my lust but to awaken my love. Keep our best interests at heart. We want to have children and grow old together." (Tob 8:5bc, 7–8)

Meditation/Journal: In what specific ways has God been a guide for you? prospered you? granted you mercy and peace?

Prayer: Blessed are you, O God of my ancestors, and blessed be your name. Throughout my life, be my guide, and prosper me. Grant me your mercy and peace today, tomorrow, and forever. Amen.

Mercy and Safety

Scripture: "When the parents had gone out and shut the door of the room, Tobias got out of bed and said to Sarah, 'Sister, get up, and let us pray and implore our Lord that he grant us mercy and safety.'" (Tob 8:4)

Reflection: On the night he is to consummate his marriage to Sarah, Tobias must remember and do two things. The first is to burn the liver and heart of the fish he caught in the Tigris River to repel the demon that has plagued Sarah. The second of Raphael's instructions is that he and Sarah are to pray to God for mercy and protection, which is what the above Scripture passage introduces. Peterson states that Tobias tells Sarah to pray for tolerance and deliverance. While the newly-wedded couple consummate their marriage, Raguel, who knows what has happened to previous sons-in-law, calls his servants, and goes with them to the family plot to dig a grave for Tobias! According to the law of Moses, he was not able to refuse the marriage of his daughter to Tobias, but he is so fearful of its outcome that he sends his wife's maid to check on the couple; the maid finds them both alive and sleeping. Because every major turning point in the novella is punctuated by a prayer, Raguel begins to pray, blessing the God of heaven who has granted mercy and protection to his daughter and son-in-law.

The marriage of Tobias and Sarah establishes a family bond between the families of Tobit and Raguel. Through their children, Tobit—whose name means *Yahweh is my good*—and Raguel—whose name means *friend of God*—are united. To mark that bond and to celebrate the mercy and protection of the Lord of heaven, Raguel prepares a two-week marriage feast! That will give Tobias time to cheer depressed Sarah and for Raguel to seal the family bond by giving half of his possessions to Tobias to take home with him. The couple's prayer for mercy and safety has been answered by the God of heaven.

Psalm Response: "Bless you, God! May every blessing, pure and simple, rain down upon you! May all your saints bless you, and all your holy creation, too; and may all your angels and your chosen ones bless you, time without end! Bless you who blessed us and turned us into joyful persons. . . . [Y]ou enfolded us in great merciful wings. Bless you who blessed these two children, our children, your children. Find a place in your heart for them as they'll find a place in their hearts for you. Fill their lives with mercy and joy." (Tob 8:15–17)

Meditation/Journal: When has God granted you mercy and safety? What bonds have been established through marriage in your family?

Prayer: Thank You, O Lord, for all the mercy and safety you have showed to me. With great compassion you have protected me and kept me safe. Continue to shower me with your blessings. All praise be to you, O God, today, tomorrow, and forever. Amen.

Finding Mercy

Scripture: Tobias prayed: "I am taking this kinswoman of mine, / not because of lust, / but with sincerity. / Grant [, O God,] that she and I may find mercy / and that we may grow old together." (Tob 8:7)

Reflection: After following Raphael's instructions about burning the liver and heart of the fish that Tobias caught in the Tigris River on the embers of incense and repelling the demon that has plagued Sarah on seven previous wedding nights, Tobias urges Sarah to get out of bed and pray that the Lord will grant them mercy and protection. After reminding God and himself that God had said that it was not good for the first man to be alone, so he created woman as a helper, Tobias tells God that he has not married Sarah because he has a strong, physical desire to have sex with her, but with honesty, integrity, and a desire to fulfill his obligation to marry her according to the law of Moses. Then, he asks that both experience divine favor, which will enable them to grow old together. After completing their prayer, they say, "Amen." Then, they go to bed, to consummate their marriage, and to sleep for the night.

Both Tobias and Sarah find God's mercy, as they both awaken the next morning. God's mercy is displayed in Raguel's order that the grave he had prepared for Tobias be filled in. God's mercy is discovered in Raguel's vow to Tobias to give him half of his possessions before Tobias heads home and the other half after he and Edna die. God's mercy is displayed in the elaborate fourteen-day marriage feast that Raguel will host for his daughter and son-in-law. Raguel's prayer that God, the Master, be merciful to Tobias and Sarah, that he keep them safe, and that he bring their lives to fulfillment in happiness and mercy is fulfilled (Tob 8:17).

Psalm Response: "Blessed are you, O Lord, God of our ancestors! You alone are praiseworthy, and your name will be blessed forever! Don't pry your mercy from our grasp; Abraham [and Sarah], your beloved friend[s], wouldn't want that, nor would his [their] son Isaac [and Rebekah] or his [their] grandson Israel [and Leah, Rachel, Bilhah, and Zilpah]. We follow you with our whole heart; fearing you still, we want to look upon your face. . . . Treat us the way you always have; massage us with your usual gentility; smother us with your inexhaustible mercy." (Dan 3:26, 35, 41 [Sg Three 1:3, 12, 19])

Meditation/Journal: What have you done recently with sincerity? What mercy from God did you find?

Prayer: O Lord, God of my ancestors, you are worthy of praise for all the mercy I have found coming from you. Do not withdraw your mercy from me; rather, give me the grace to follow you and to seek your presence. In your abundant mercy, hear my prayer. Amen.

Apocrypha/Deuterocanonicals

Great Mercy 1

Scripture: Raguel prayed: "Blessed are you [, O God,] because you have made me glad. It has not turned out as I expected, / but you have dealt with us according to your great mercy." (Tob 8:16)

Reflection: The above verse is part of a prayer recited by Raguel after he and his servants have finished digging a grave for Tobias and, at a maid's word, discovered that Tobias did not die on his wedding night, like his wife Sarah's previous seven husbands! God, according to Raguel, has watched over Tobias (in the person of Raphael) and made Raguel glad, because Tobias did not die during his wedding night. As can be determined by his action of digging a grave, Raguel expected Tobias to die on his wedding night, just like the seven previous husbands. Instead, God has treated Tobias, Raguel, Edna, and Sarah according to his great mercy, that is, his magnanimous generosity. Tobias remains alive. Raguel and Edna now have a son-in-law. Sarah now has a living husband! A dug grave will receive no body!

The narrator of the story informs the reader that Raguel has undergone a great change. He expected that Tobias would die during the night—after all, the usual scenario for seven times was the discovery of the death of Sarah's husband—but Tobias is alive. God has had compassion on his children: Tobias and Sarah. Raguel's change is indicated by the order given to his servants to fill in the grave intended for Tobias' body before daybreak (Tob 8:18), his request to Edna to bake many loaves of bread (Tob 8:19), and his choosing of two steers and four rams (Tob 8:19) for a fourteen-day feast! In other words, the great or, according to NAB, abundant, mercy of God turned Raguel's world upside-down! God's mercy is greater than Raguel could expect.

Psalm Response: ". . . [W]e bless the Lord; we praise and honor him forever. / For he rescued us from the world below and saved us from the hand of death . . . . / Stand up and proclaim the greatness of the Lord; he is goodness itself and his mercy never quits. All who are in awe of the God of gods, bless the Lord; stand up and proclaim him, for his mercy never quits." (Dan 3:88–90 [Sg Three 1:66–68])

Meditation/Journal: What great (abundant, unexpected) mercy have you received from God? What change did it spark in you?

Prayer: God of heaven, every pure blessing comes from you. You give me great delight when you turn my expectations upside-down with your unexpected mercy. Grant that my experience of your abundant blessings lead me to change my perspectives and my life today, tomorrow, and forever. Amen.

Happiness and Mercy

Scripture: "Blessed are you [, O God,] because you had compassion / on two only children. / Be merciful to them, O Master, and keep them safe; / bring their lives to fulfillment / in happiness and mercy." (Tob 8:17)

Reflection: The above verse, part of Raguel's prayer after discovering that his son-in-law, Tobias, did not die during his wedding night with Raguel's daughter, Sarah, mentions God's compassion, his sympathy for the suffering of others. In this story, God demonstrates compassion directly to Tobias and Sarah—keeping them alive—and indirectly to Raguel and Edna—keeping alive their son-in-law and daughter. For seven past wedding nights, Sarah, Raguel, and Edna found Sarah's husband—and Raguel and Edna's son-in-law—dead! Raguel's prayer mentions that Tobias is Tobit and Anna's only son, and Sarah is Raguel and Edna's only daughter. God's compassion means more to the parents of only one child.

Then, God, the Master, is petitioned to continue to show mercy to Tobias and Sarah by keeping them safe. Peterson asks God to find a place in his heart for them, as they find a place in their hearts for him. NAB asks God to protect them. Raguel asks God to bring their lives to fulfillment, that is, to give them a long life together in happiness—joyful and satisfied pleasure—and mercy—without distress or pain. After finishing his prayer, Raguel orders his servants to fill in before daybreak the grave they dug the night before (Tob 8:9b–10, 18).

Psalm Response: "'If you'll hold on to me for dear life,' says GOD, / 'I'll get you out of any trouble. I'll give you the best of care / if you'll only get to know and trust me. / Call me and I'll answer, be at your side in bad times; / I'll rescue you, then throw you a party. / I'll give you a long life, / give you a long drink of salvation.'" (Ps 91:14–16)

Meditation/Journal: What happiness and mercy have you experienced from God? What long-life fulfillment have you experienced from God?

Prayer: O God, you demonstrate your power by showing mercy to your people. Bestow your compassion upon me, protect me, give me a long life, and complete what you have begun in me. Amen.

Merciful Light

Scripture: Tobit prayed: "Blessed be God, / and blessed be his great name, / and blessed be all his holy angels. / May his holy name be blessed / throughout all the ages. / Though he afflicted me, / he has had mercy upon me. / Now I see my son Tobias!" (Tob 11:14b–15)

Reflection: While Tobias and Sarah are enjoying the two-week wedding feast that Raguel and Edna are hosting for them, Tobias sends Azariah (Raphael) to get the money, which was the original reason for leaving Nineveh in the first place (Tob 9:1–6). Meanwhile, in Nineveh, Tobit and Anna await Tobias' return (Tob 10:1–7a). Once the fourteen-day wedding banquet is completed, Tobias and Sarah and Azariah (Raphael) begin their journey to Nineveh (Tob 10:7b–13). Outside Nineveh Raphael reminds Tobias that the gall from the fish he caught in the Tigris River will heal his blind father, Tobit, if it is smeared on his eyes. Leaving Sarah at the city gate, Tobias and Raphael go to Tobit's home, greet Anna, and, after greeting Tobit, Tobias smears the medicine (gall) on Tobit's eyes and peels off the white films that have caused Tobias' blindness. At last, Tobit can see his son, and, hugging him, declares that he is the light of his eyes (Tob 11:1–14a).

At this point in the novella, the second healing (the first being Sarah's) has been accomplished. The reader must keep in mind the meaning of the name Raphael: God heals. Azariah, Raphael in disguise, is God traveling among his people in a foreign land, displaying his mercy, and healing them. Tobit responds to this second healing with the fifth prayer in the book. In his prayer, Tobit attributes both affliction and healing to God, because God oversees everything. Affliction is viewed as a part of the divine plan to heal, to bring together people, and, in so doing, to shower them with merciful blessings—in Tobit's healing, to shower him with merciful light. After the prayer, all that is left to do is for Tobit and Anna to go with Tobias, who has given his father the money he went to retrieve (Tob 11:15c), to the city gate and welcome their daughter-in-law Sarah to Nineveh (Tob 11:16–18).

Psalm Response: "Blessed be God! Blessed be his great name! Blessed be all the holy angels forever! He's the one who laid the lash on me more than once, but he's also the one who returned my son to me!" (Tob 11:14b–15)

Meditation/Journal: When have you experienced God traveling with you? What merciful light did God shine on you? Do you attribute both affliction and healing to God? Explain.

Prayer: I bless your great name, O God, and I praise you for all your works. Make me more aware of your healing presence, and help me to understand your mysterious work in my life today, tomorrow, and forever. Amen.

Mercy Showed 1

Scripture: "... Tobit said: 'Blessed be God who lives forever, / because his kingdom lasts throughout all ages. / For he afflicts, and he shows mercy; / he leads down to Hades in the lowest regions of the earth; / and he brings up from the great abyss, / and there is nothing that can escape his hand.'" (Tob 13:1–2)

Reflection: After Tobit and Anna host a wedding celebration for Tobias and Sarah in Nineveh, Azariah (Raphael) re-enters the narrative. Tobit and Tobias agree that he should be paid half of the money Tobias and Azariah retrieved, because he was a good guide for Tobias, cured Sarah, retrieved the money, and cured Tobit (Tob 12:1–5). Raphael reveals that his mission from God has been to heal Sarah and Tobit (Tob 12:14). "I am Raphael," he states, "one of the seven angels who stand ready and enter before the glory of the Lord" (Tob 12:15). He reveals that he has been acting by God's will. Then, because he is God, a spirit, an angel, he disappears from their sight. "... [W]hat you saw was a vision ... ," he tells them (Tob 12:19). Raphael's departure leads Tobit to voice a seventeen-verse hymn of praise, of which the first two verses are found in the Scripture text above.

In this sixth formal prayer of the book, Tobit proclaims God's mercy. The basis for God's mercy is God's power, which accomplishes all things. First, God lives forever. Second, his kingdom exists throughout all time. Third, he afflicts and shows compassion or sympathy for people's sufferings. Fourth, from the perspective of a three-storied universe, he can lead to Hades—the Greek underworld, equivalent to the Hebrew Sheol—and he can bring back to the second-story earth those in the great abyss—the Greek abode of the dead. Nothing can escape God's power! In other words, the all-powerful God shows mercy—kindness, forgiveness, compassion—to those over whom he has power. He shows mercy out of his generosity.

Psalm Response: "Bless the living God forever, / Bless all his kingdom. / Both merciless and merciful, / he's the highway to Hades and back. / Swiping us from the jaws of hell, / his majesty saves us from our travesty. / No one escapes the movements of his hand." (Tob 13:1–2)

Meditation/Journal: In what specific experience of your life has God showed mercy to you? What power did God display?

Prayer: Blessed are you, O God, because you live forever. Your power is seen in the mercy you show to everyone and everything you have created. Show your merciful power to me today, tomorrow, and forever. Amen.

Mercy Showed 2

Scripture: Tobit prayed: God "has shown you [children of Isael] his greatness [among the nations]. / Exalt him in the presence of every living being, / because he is our Lord and he is our God; / he is our Father and he is God forever. / He will afflict you for your iniquities, / but he will again show mercy on all of you. / He will gather you from all the nations / among whom you have been scattered." (Tob 13:4–5)

Reflection: The OT (A) novella named Tobit is set after the fall of the Northern Kingdom of Israel to Assyria in 722 BCE and the deportation of the people to Nineveh. The prayer Tobit voices after his son, Tobias, heals his blindness draws a parallel between Tobit's suffering and deliverance and the suffering and hoped-for deliverance of the exiles. Verses 4 and 5 above, taken from the seventeen-verse hymn found in chapter 13 of the book of Tobit, illustrate the mercy God bestows out of his great power. Just as Tobit was afflicted with blindness and, receiving God's mercy, had his sight restored, so the children of Israel, scattered among the nations, have been showed God's mercy and have the opportunity, in turn, to display it before the nations where they live as exiles. Others will see them exalting God, their Lord and Father, and acknowledge his eternity, kingdom, and power to show mercy.

Because all power belongs to God, it is he who afflicts the exiles for their iniquities (Deut 4:25–40; 28:1–68). However, Tobit's hymn expresses the hope that God will show mercy again by gathering the exiles out of the nations among whom they have been scattered. Tobit's song echoes Isaiah's words about the Judahites' return from Babylonian exile to Jerusalem (Isa 54:11–12; 60:1–14; 66:10–14) along with the prophet Micah's words about many nations coming to the LORD's house to be taught his ways (Mic 4:1–2) and the prophet Zechariah's words about many strong nations seeking the LORD of hosts (Zech 8:22). The author of Tobit knows the prophetic hope imbedded in biblical books, and he expresses it through Tobit's hymn, which was most likely not a part of the original book, but added at a different time. In other words, once Azariah reveals himself to be Raphael, the plot of the novella—the healing of Sarah and Tobit—is concluded.

Psalm Response: "Confess [God] to the Gentiles, children of Israel, / even though he's led you into the wilderness. / Exalt him in front of every living being; / he's your Lord, your Father, / your God for all time. / He laid the lash on your shoulders, / but he rubbed balm in your wounds; / he rounded you up from among the Gentiles, / wherever you were lost in the crowd." (Tob 13:3–5)

Meditation/Journal: What divine greatness has God showed you? What powerful mercy has God showed you? Has God ever afflicted you because of your iniquities? Explain.

Prayer: I give you thanks, O God, for the divine greatness you have displayed by showing mercy to me. I exalt you, Lord, for being my Father, and I place all my hope in you to be drawn to you forever and ever. Amen.

Turn for Mercy

Scripture: O children of Israel, "If you turn to [God] with all your heart and with all your soul, to do what is true before him, / then he will turn to you / and will no longer hide his face from you. / So now see what he has done for you; / acknowledge him at the top of your voice. / Bless the Lord of righteousness, / and exalt the King of the ages. / In the land of my exile I acknowledge him, / and show his power and majesty to a nation of sinners: / 'Turn back, you sinners, and do what is right before him; / perhaps he may look with favor upon you and show you mercy.'" (Tob 13:6)

Apocrypha/Deuterocanonicals

Reflection: In verse 6 above of the thirteen-verse hymn prayed by Tobit after his blindness is healed and most likely added to the OT (A) book after it was finished, the word *turn* occurs three times. First, Tobit exhorts the children of Israel to turn to God with all their heart and spirit; the exhortation echoes similar words in the prophet Jeremiah (3:12-14; 22—4:1), which employs the word *return* several times. Second, Tobit states that the turning of the children of Israel will result in the turning of God to them, words echoing the prophet Zechariah (1:3). God turning toward the children of Israel and no longer hiding his face is not to be understood literally; the phrases are metaphors to emphasize that God will once again favor his people with mercy. Third, Tobit refers to the children of Israel as sinners, who need to turn back and do what is right in the hope that God will show them mercy. To turn or to return means to face a different direction; while the turn or return may be interpreted literally, it implies a different direction mentally. In other words, the Israelites need to change their minds, which will change their behavior.

The turning of the children of Israel, according to Tobit's hymn, begins by acknowledging all that God has done for them as loud as they can. While it may be hard for a people in exile to begin to think positively about all that God has done for them, that is exactly the point of the song. Exile becomes a negative experience only when it is separated from God. If the exiles begin their prayer with God overseeing everything, then all that has happened to them, including exile, is a work of God. And everything God does is right; therefore, the King of the ages should be exalted. Tobit, in Assyria, the land of his exile, acknowledges God, states that he has turned toward him, and announces the mercy that flows from God's power. Just like Tobit prepares to receive more of God's mercy, the author of the CB (NT) letter of Jude tells his readers to "look forward to the mercy of our Lord Jesus Christ that leads to eternal life" (Jude 1:21).

Psalm Response: "My head is high, GOD, held high; / I'm looking to you, GOD . . . . / I've thrown in my lot with you; / You won't embarrass me, will you? / Or let my enemies get the best of me? / Show me how you work, GOD; / School me in your ways. / GOD is fair and just; / He corrects the misdirected, / Sends them in the right direction. / He gives the rejects his hand, / And leads them step-by-step. (Ps 25:1-4, 8-9)

Meditation/Journal: Most recently, when have you (re)turned to God and discovered that he had (re)turned to you to favor you with mercy? About what did you change your mind that led to a change in behavior? What did you first consider negatively that became a positive work of God?

Prayer: Lord of all righteousness, King of the ages, you demonstrate your power by showing mercy to your people, who, listening to your prophets, return to you. I exalt you for all you have done for me, and I ask you to show me your face. I shout this prayer loudly and clearly today, tomorrow, and forever. Amen.

Have Mercy

Scripture: "O Jerusalem, the holy city, / [God] afflicted you for the deeds of your hands, / but will again have mercy on the children of the righteous. / Acknowledge the Lord, for he is good, / and bless the King of the ages, / so that his tent may be rebuilt in you in joy. / May he cheer all those within you who are captives, / and love all those within you who are distressed, to all generations forever." (Tob 13:9–10)

Reflection: The second half of Tobit's hymn (Tob 14:1–17), verses 9 through 17, is a song about Jerusalem. The passage above comes from the first two verses about Jerusalem. While the Assyrians never captured Jerusalem, they did lay siege to the holy city in 701 BCE. In 720 BCE, they captured Samaria, the capital of the Northern Kingdom of Israel, and deported over 27,000 Israelites; it is at that time that the OT (A) book of Tobit is set. Sennacherib, king of the Assyrians, besieged Jerusalem, but he did not capture it; according to the Bible, his army was struck with an epidemic that caused him to withdraw and that saved the city. However, Jerusalem fell to King Nebuchadnezzar of Babylon in 587 BCE. The fall of Jerusalem in 587 BCE has influenced the writer of chapter 13 of the book of Tobit in the third to second century BCE. Chapter 13 was not originally a part of the book; it was added at a date later than the composition of the first twelve chapters of the book. A reading of the book of Tobit indicates that the book originally ended at 12:22, after the plot was resolved.

The influence of the fall of Jerusalem to Nebuchadnezzar is seen in the words about rebuilding God's tent, a reference to the Temple that was destroyed by Nebuchadnezzar, who left the poor, sick, and aged as distressed captives in Jerusalem and took every able-bodied man, woman, and child as captives to Babylon. Also, the author of Tobit's hymn is familiar with the prophet Isaiah (60:1–22), as can be seen in his reference to light (Tob 13:11), gifts being brought to rebuilt Jerusalem (Tob 13:11, 16–17), the mention of the walls being destroyed (Tob 13:12), and more. Of particular importance here is the mercy God shows to the children of the righteous (Tob 13:9), which echoes the favorable mercy the LORD has in Isaiah (60:10).

Psalm Response: "O Jerusalem, holiest of cities . . . / Your reputation . . . will last forever. / Happy are those who love you, O Jerusalem, / and happy are those who rejoice in your peace. / My soul, bless the Lord, the great King; / he'll build his house in Jerusalem, / and it will last until the end of the world. / Bless the God of Israel, / bless those who bless his name / from here to eternity. (Tob 13:9a, 11b, 13b, 15, 18b)

Meditation/Journal: Why do you think one biblical author added to another biblical author's work? What city do you think has received God's mercy? Explain. Why was Jerusalem so important to the biblical world?

Prayer: Your servant David, O Lord, chose Jerusalem to be his capital city and brought the ark of your presence into it and placed it under a tent. Your servant Solomon built the first Temple in the holy city, and you chose to live in the building he erected. Have mercy on all who live in Jerusalem, and keep all of them in peace today, tomorrow, and forever. Amen.

Mercy Again

Scripture: "When he was about to die, [Tobit] called his son Tobias and the seven sons of Tobias and gave this command: 'My son, take your children and hurry off to Media . . . . Indeed, everything that was spoken by the prophets of Israel, whom God sent, will occur. None of all their words will fail, but all will come true at their appointed times. So it will be safer in Media than in Assyria and Babylon. All of our kindred, inhabitants of the land of Israel, will be scattered and taken as captives from the good land; and the whole land of Israel will be desolate, even Samaria and Jerusalem will be desolate. And the temple of God in it will be burned to the ground, and it will be desolate for a while. But God will again have mercy on them and God will bring them back into the land of Israel; and they will rebuild the temple of God, but not like the first one until the period of when the times of fulfillment shall come.'" (Tob 14:3–4aef, 5a)

Reflection: Like chapter 13, chapter 14 was added to the OT (A) book of Tobit. The chapter has nothing to do with the story told in chapters 1 through 12. It was composed after the Persians, Medes, and Babylonians conquered Assyria and Nineveh in 612 BCE and King Nebuchadnezzar of Babylon moved on to conquer Judah and Jerusalem in 587 BCE. The author predicts that Jerusalem and its Temple will be destroyed; that is a safe prediction because it had already happened when he was writing in the third to second century BCE! He also predicts the return of the captives and the rebuilding of the Temple; that, too, is a safe prediction because the first group of Jews left exile and returned to the holy city in 538 BCE. The author of chapter 14 knows that God did show mercy again; the biblical authors interpret the conquest of Babylon by King Cyrus of Persia, who permitted the Jews to return to Jerusalem, as an act of God's mercy again (2 Chr 36:20, 22–23).

Furthermore, the author of chapter 14, as indicated above, knows the prophets. Clear allusions to Zechariah 8:20–23 can be found, and Isaiah 40:1—55:13, the renewal of hope for Jerusalem and comfort offered to scattered Israel, are echoed. Nineveh's defeat by Babylon is seen as punishment for Nineveh's defeat of Israel. Babylon's defeat by Persia is seen as punishment for Babylon's defeat of Judah and Jerusalem. Biblical retribution holds that the righteous flourish, while the wicked are punished. This is true, biblically, because God shows mercy again and again, and many of the verses of the OT (A) book of Tobit drip with God's mercy!

Psalm Response: "Help us again, God of our help; / don't hold a grudge against us forever. / You aren't going to keep this up, are you? / scowling and angry, year after year? / Why not help us make a fresh start—a resurrection life? / *Then* your people will laugh and sing! / Show us how much you love us, GOD! / Give us the salvation we need!" (Ps 85:4–7)

Meditation/Journal: How often (again) does God show mercy to you? What do you think about biblical retribution—the righteous flourish and the wicked are punished?

Prayer: O God, I thirst for you, the living God, who has mercy on me again and again. As I praise you, my help and my God, I ask that you lift my spirit again with your abundant mercy. Hear my prayer today, tomorrow, and forever. Amen.

APOCRYPHA/DEUTEROCANONICALS

Show no Mercy

Scripture: ". . . Nebuchadnezzar, king of the Assyrians, called Holofernes, the chief general of his army, second only to himself, and said to him, 'Thus says the Great King, the lord of the whole earth: . . . March out against all the land to the west, because they disobeyed my order. I will lead them away captive to the ends of the whole earth. But to those who resist show no mercy, but hand them over to slaughter and plunder throughout your whole region.'" (Jdt 2:4-6, 9, 11)

Reflection: The OT (A) book of Judith is a novella, written in the middle of the second century BCE. It narrates the story of a powerful evil empire versus a weak warrior woman. The evil empire is headed by King Nebuchadnezzar, historically King of Babylon; here he is King of Assyria. In other words, the two worst empires in Jewish history have been combined to create a fictitious evil empire, commanded by Holofernes, who is presented like a prophet commanded by God! Moreover, Nebuchadnezzar refers to himself as lord of the whole earth, which raises the question: Who is lord of the whole earth? The warrior woman is Judith, meaning *Jewess*, from a mountain town named Bethulia, which means *virgin*!

To show how powerful the evil empire is, the author of the book of Judith portrays Nebuchadnezzar telling Holofernes to show no mercy to those who resist his rule. Here, mercy refers to leniency; no gentleness or tolerance is to be showed to resisters. They are to be killed and their property plundered. After his audience with the king, Holofernes begins his campaign (Jdt 2:14). While the people of the seacoast surrender (Jdt 2:28—3:9), the Israelites living in Judah prepare for the attack (Jdt 4:1-15). Holofernes gathers information about Israel from Achior, leader of all the Ammonites (Jdt 5:1-24), after which he is banished to Bethulia (Jdt 6:1-13). The people of Bethulia hear what Achior has to say; then, they call upon the God of Israel for help (Jdt 6:14-21). Meanwhile, Holofernes prepares his army to march on Bethulia and lay siege to it (Jdt 7:1-18). The Israelites know that Holofernes shows no mercy; so they prepare to surrender to him (Jdt 7:19-32). Judith, however, knows that "judgment will be without mercy to anyone who has shown no mercy; mercy triumphs over judgment" (Jas 2:13).

Psalm Response: "I look to you, heaven-dwelling God, / look up to you for help. / Like servants, alert to their master's commands, / like a maiden attending her lady, / We're watching and waiting, holding our breath, / awaiting your word of mercy. / Mercy, GOD, mercy! / We've been kicked around long enough ...." (Ps 123:1–3)

Meditation/Journal: Have you ever experienced Nebuchadnezzar's show-no-mercy policy from another person? Explain. Most recently, when have you sought mercy from God?

Prayer: God of abundant mercy, even when people show no mercy to each other, you display gentleness and tolerance to all. Hear my prayer for those who show no mercy; fill them with your generous grace that overflows into clemency, pardon, and patience today, tomorrow, and forever. Amen.

Mercy Turned Again

Scripture: "... [A]ll the people [of Bethulia], the young men, the women, and the children, gathered around Uzziah and the rulers of the town and cried out with a loud voice, and said before the elders, 'Let God judge between you and us! You have done us a great injury in not making peace with the Assyrians. For now we have no one to help us ....' But Uzziah said to them, 'Courage, my brothers and sisters! Let us hold out for five days more; by that time the Lord our God will turn his mercy to us again, for he will not forsake us utterly.'" (Jdt 7:23–25, 30)

Reflection: Once the Assyrian army, under the leadership of Holofernes, encamps near Bethulia and prepares to lay siege to the town, the Israelites, seeing their great number, are terrified (Jdt 7:1–18). Uzziah, the chief elder of Bethulia, reminds his fellow citizens that their desire to surrender to the Assyrians (Jdt 7:19–32), needs to be tweaked. That is why Uzziah proposes a more moderate position of waiting for five days to see if God will deliver them. Uzziah chooses five days because five, used over three hundred times in biblical literature, is a sacred number; it refers to Moses' five books of the Torah—Genesis, Exodus, Leviticus, Numbers, Deuteronomy—and, in the CB (NT) Gospel of Matthew, it refers to the new Moses, Jesus', five discourses (sermons). The HB (OT) book of Psalms is divided into five parts. Five represents God's grace, goodness, mercy, and unmerited gift. Often, the number appears in the ages of biblical characters; Judith lived to be 105 (Jdt 16:23). In the CB (NT), the Markan Jesus feeds five thousand people with five loaves of bread. Five or any of its multiples is a referent to God's abundance, grace, goodness, mercy, and gift.

Therefore, it comes as no surprise that Judith, who feared God with great devotion (Jdt 8:8), appears in the story! After upbraiding the citizens of Bethulia for their decision to surrender to Holofernes (Jdt 8:9–27), she prays (Jdt 9:1–14), and she presents an alternative plan (Jdt 10:1–10) and puts it into action (Jdt 10:11–23). The mercy that God will turn to his people again comes from a very unlikely biblical source; it is not a man; it is not the elders of the city; it is not an army; it is a woman: Judith! She is the means. She prays: "Give to me, a widow, the strong hand to do what I plan" (Jdt 9:9b).

Psalm Response: "Hear my prayer, God of my father, God of the Israelites, Dominator of all things, Creator of the waters, King of the universe; hear my prayer! May my silken words whispered into the enemies' ears cause ruin among their ranks. Let your whole nation and the tribes that compose it know that you're the God of Universal Power and Might and not just one of those random rulers that come along from time to time." (Jdt 9:12–13a, 14)

Meditation/Journal: When have you experienced God turning again to you with mercy? Explain. What was its unlikely source?

Prayer: Lord, you are the God of my ancestors, to whom you turned and showed mercy again and again. Make me the recipient of your mercy by giving me the strength to know your will and to do it in praise of your might today, tomorrow, and forever. Amen.

Mercy Showed 3

Scripture: "I will sing to my God a new song; O Lord, you are great and glorious, / wonderful in strength, invincible. / Let all your creatures serve you, / for you spoke, and they were made. / You sent forth your spirit, and it formed them; / there is none that can resist your voice. / For the mountains shall be shaken to their foundations with the waters; / before your glance the rocks shall melt like wax. / But to those who fear you / you show mercy." (Jdt 16:13–15)

Reflection: Because she is beautiful, Judith's plan is to sneak into the Assyrian camp and trick Holofernes, who invites her into his tent to dine with him. After he drinks too much wine and falls asleep, she takes his sword and beheads him. Then, she and the maid she brought with her take his head to Bethulia, where it is hung on the city wall. When the Assyrians see it, they flee the area in fear, and the Israelites plunder what the army leaves behind (Jdt 10:1—15:13). Then, Judith sings a victory song, from where the verses in the above Scripture passage are taken. In the first half of the hymn (Jdt 16:1-12), Judith calls upon the citizens of Bethulia to worship God as victor and deliverer; in other words, God has won the victory through the woman named Judith!

In the second half of the hymn (Jdt 16:13-17), Judith praises God with a new song; she summons all creation to join her in praise. Those people who fear, (reverence), God, are entitled to his mercy. Judith declares that every sacrifice's fragrant offering is a small thing and the fat of every burnt offering is a very little thing in comparison to those who fear the Lord; they are great forever (Jdt 16:16); in other words, Judith is great because God has made her great with his mercy. Those who rise against the Lord Almighty's people, like Holofernes (and Nebuchadnezzar), suffer ruin (Jdt 16:17), which is the point of the novella! Then, just as she suddenly entered the novella, Judith exits the work. The courage she showed when facing Holofernes, results in mercy showed to the citizens of Bethulia (Jdt 16:18-24). According to the novelist, "No one ever gain spread terror among the Israelites during the lifetime of Judith, or for a long time after her death" (Jdt 16:25).

Psalm Response: "It was the Most High who blessed you and made you first among women on the face of the earth. Yes, it was he—the one who created Heaven and earth—who directed your hand to do the bloody deed. May your praise never leave the hearts of humankind, who will remember the strength of our God forever and ever. May God exalt the memory of your risking your life for your people, even when they'd been humiliated by their enemies. You diverted our ruin while remaining in the straight and narrow yourself." (Jdt 13:18-20)

Meditation/Journal: What woman do (have) you know(n) who feared God and was the means for God to show mercy to others? Explain.

Prayer: Most High God, you bless those who reverence you with your abundant mercy. As I remember your power, Lord, show mercy to me. Send your Spirit to guide my steps on your path and give me the strength to praise you today, tomorrow, and forever. Amen.

Apocrypha/Deuterocanonicals

Mercy on Inheritance

Scripture: "'... Mordecai prayed to the Lord, calling to remembrance all the works of the Lord. [He said:] '... O Lord God and King, God of Abraham, spare your people; for the eyes of our foes are upon us to annihilate us, and they desire to destroy the inheritance that has been yours from the beginning. Do not neglect your portion, which you redeemed for yourself out of Egypt. Hear my prayer, and have mercy upon your inheritance; turn our mourning into feasting that we may live and sing praise to your name, O Lord....'" (Esth 13:8, 15–17 [Add Esth C:1, 8–10a])

Reflection: There are three known versions of the HB (OT) book of Esther. The Hebrew version differs from the Greek version. The various versions reflect the concerns of the writers and the religious communities for whom they are writing. The book is set at the time of Artaxerxes the Great, successor to King Nebuchadnezzar of Babylon, who is enthroned in Susa. Mordecai, a Jew, living in Susa, has fostered his niece, Esther, who, after Queen Vashti refused to obey her husband, the king, was gathered with other young women to find a new queen for the king; ultimately, Esther is chosen as the new queen. Meanwhile, Haman, one of Artaxerxes "Friends" was advanced by the king to first place. After Mordecai refused to bow to him, Haman hatched a plot by casting lots to deceive the king into decreeing that the Jews be destroyed. Mordecai informs Esther of the plot, telling her that it was for such a time as this that she was made queen (Esth 4:14). Then, Mordecai prays to the Lord for help. The above Scripture text is part of Mordecai's prayer.

Because the Jews are in Babylonian captivity and about to be destroyed by Haman, Mordecai acknowledges that no one can oppose the Lord when it is his will to save Israel (Esth 13:9 [Add Esth C:2]). Then, recalling that the Lord was Abraham's God, he asks God to spare his people, who are about to be annihilated. He asks God to have mercy on the people he once led out of Egypt; he asks that his prayer be heard and that God show pity (NAB) upon his inheritance. Mordecai echoes a familiar theme in a lament, such as his prayer is, that God must spare his people so that they can declare his praises. After Mordecai finishes his prayer, Queen Esther prays in a similar way. As the narrative progresses, Esther foils Haman's plans by convincing Artaxerxes to spare her people and to hang Haman on the very gallows he had prepared to hang the Jews. Then, a new decree is issued that cancels Haman's plans. Mordecai says, "These things have come from God"

(Esth 10:4 [Add Esth F:1]). In other words, God has showed mercy on his inheritance.

Psalm Response: "God! Barbarians have broken into your home, / violated your holy temple, / left Jerusalem a pile of rubble! / You're famous for helping; God, give *us* a break. / Your reputation is on the line. / Pull us out of this mess, forgive us our sins— / do what you're famous for doing!" (Ps 79:1, 9)

Meditation/Journal: What mercy showed you (God's inheritance) have you experienced? Whom did you tell about your experience? How did you praise God?

Prayer: O God, when I find myself lamenting my condition, I turn to you for mercy. Send help to me. You, who rule over all, make my days full of joy and gladness, and I will praise you today, tomorrow, and forever. Amen.

Grace and Mercy 1

Scripture: "In the time of the [righteous'] visitation they will shine forth, / and will run like sparks through the stubble. / Those who trust in [God] will understand truth, / and the faithful will abide with him in love, / because grace and mercy are upon his holy ones, / and he watches over his elect." (Wis 3:7, 9)

Reflection: In the usual manner of biblical thinking, the future of all beyond the grave was the same weak and pale existence in the underworld, named Sheol, separated from God. However, in the OT (A) book of Wisdom, the author proposes that a separation takes place between the righteous and the unrighteous after death. The just are in the hand of God (Wis 3:1) and the wicked go to Sheol, considered a place of torment (Wis 4:18–19). At the time of divine intervention or judgment after death, the righteous will shine and be like sparks setting stubble on fire. The image of light is one of triumph, as is found in the prophet Daniel: "Those who are wise shall shine like the brightness of the sky, and those who lead many to righteousness, like the stars forever and ever" (Dan 12:3). Those who trust God have knowledge of God and possess heavenly wisdom; their destiny is life with God. Indeed, they understand truth; because they are faithful; according to Peterson, they will enjoy eternal rest. God showers grace—himself—and mercy—compassion—on those committed to him. According to Peterson, he even drops in for a personal chat with them from time to time! Those who are faithful abide with God in love, states NAB. The spirits of the just commune with the Spirit of God.

The phrases about God's grace and mercy being upon his holy ones and that God watches over his elect are also found in Wisdom 4:15: ". . . God's grace and mercy are with his elect, and . . . he watches over his holy ones." The righteous enjoy God's gift (favor) of himself to them, and they accept his gift, which strengthens them to remain true to the trust they place in him. They also accepted his compassion, kindness, and forgiveness; they did not choose God; God chose them. By sharing himself with the righteous, he made them his holy ones (saints); he watches over all those he has chosen or elected. The faithful experience God's divine existence in love. In the CB (NT), the Johannine Jesus emphasizes the same idea, stating, "If you abide in me, and my words abide in you, ask for whatever you wish, and it will be done for you. . . . [Y[ou will abide in my love, just as I . . . abide in [my Father's] love" (John 15:7, 10).

Psalm Response: "Keep company with God, / get in on the best. / Open up before GOD, keep nothing back; he'll do whatever needs to be done; / He'll validate your life in the clear light of day / and stamp you with approval at high noon. / Less is more and more is less. / One righteous will outclass fifty wicked, / For the wicked are moral weaklings, / but the righteous are GOD-strong. / GOD keeps track of the decent folk; / what they do won't soon be forgotten." (Ps 37:4-6, 16-18)

Meditation/Journal: What specific grace and mercy have you received from God? What is the love you share (abide in) with God like?

Prayer: Because you chose me, O God, I abide in love with you, as you bestow your grace and mercy upon me. Never cease to watch over me, and, at the time of my death, grant that my spirit be united with your Spirit forever. Amen.

Grace and Mercy 2

Scripture: "Being perfected in a short time, [those who pleased God and were loved by him] fulfilled long years; / for their souls were pleasing to the Lord, / therefore he took them quickly from the midst of wickedness. / Yet the peoples saw and did not understand, / or take such a thing to heart, /

that God's grace and mercy are with his elect, / and that he watches over his holy ones." (Wis 4:13–15)

Reflection: The Jewish perspective was that the wicked die young and a long life was a blessing from God; the old die at an honorable age. The author of the OT (A) book of Wisdom challenges that view. He writes that God chooses to perfect some who please him and love him in a short time; however, their early deaths do not indicate that they were wicked. Rather, according to the author, because their spirits were pleasing to the Lord, he took them to himself to rescue them from contamination. In other words, those pleasing to God may die young, but they were quickly perfected (Wis 4:16b). In the words of Billy Joel, maybe only the good die young!

After proposing a new way of thinking about the good dying young, the author reflects on how many people have witnessed a young person's death and did not possess the wisdom to reflect upon the fact that God's grace and mercy were with those he had chosen (Wis 4:17). The supreme God cannot be controlled by people. The Lord showers holiness on his holy ones; he watches over those he has graced with himself. He shows them his compassion, kindness, and generosity. Thus, like Enoch, who walked with God and was taken by God (Gen 5:24), there are young people who please God, are loved by him, and taken by him to himself; they are selected to receive grace and mercy. Physical death is not the end of existence; according to the author of Wisdom, spirit is joined to Spirit, who is God.

Psalm Reflection: "O my soul, bless GOD. / From head to toe, I'll bless his holy name! / O my soul, bless GOD, / don't forget a single blessing! / He renews your youth—you're always young in his presence. / GOD makes everything come out right; / he puts victims back on their feet." (Ps 103:1–2, 5–6)

Meditation/Journal: What person did you know who was pleasing to God and received grace and mercy and died young? What cultural presuppositions do you have about such biblical notions as the wicked die young, long life is a blessing from God, and God takes people to himself?

Prayer: Help me to understand your ways, O God, and fill me with your grace and mercy. Bring to perfection what you have begun in me, that I may be pleasing in your sight. Keep watch over me today, tomorrow, and forever. Amen.

Apocrypha/Deuterocanonicals

Pardoned in Mercy

Scripture: "... [T]he lowliest may be pardoned in mercy, / but the mighty will be mightily tested. For the Lord of all will not stand in awe of anyone, / or show deference to greatness; / because he himself made both small and great, / and he takes thought for all alike." (Wis 6:6–7)

Reflection: The author of the OT (A) book of Wisdom addresses all rulers—kings, judges, etc.—about the importance of learning wisdom. The wisdom to be learned by rulers is that their authority or sovereignty comes from the Lord, who inquires about their works and plans. If such rulers do not keep the law themselves or walk according to God's purpose, he will judge them severely. While God may pardon in mercy the lowliest of people—those who are not rulers—the mighty will be judged carefully. Unlike the lowly who stand in awe of rulers, God does not admire anyone; he shows no deference or partiality to those he has made great. And the Lord thinks about rulers in the same way as he thinks about everyone else. No one gets preferred treatment from God, states the author of Wisdom.

Those in the lower classes, according to the author of Wisdom, may be pardoned in mercy by God. To pardon is to release or forgive for wrongdoing; it is to set free a person from punishment. God forgives the lowly out of his generosity, because he has power over all, according to Wisdom's author. However, he holds accountable those to whom he has entrusted authority, such as presidents, prime ministers, managers, bosses, etc. Because God is the final judge, the tone set by the author is one of warning.

Psalm Response: "Praise GOD from heaven, / praise him from the mountaintops; / Praise, oh let them praise the name of GOD— / he spoke the word, and there they were! / Praise GOD from earth, Earth's kings and all races, / leaders and important people, / Robust men and women in their prime, / and yes, graybeards and little children." (Ps 148:1b, 5, 7a, 11–12)

Meditation/Journal: When has God pardoned you in mercy? Do you think God judges those in authority severely? Explain. Who has authority over you? Make a list.

Prayer: I seek your wisdom, O God. I seek to do what is right before you, Most High. Help me to walk according to your purpose and all along the way pardon me in mercy. Make me holy as I observe holy things in holiness today, tomorrow, and forever. Amen.

Disciplined in Mercy

Scripture: "When [the Israelites] were thirsty, they called upon you [, O Lord,], / and water was given them out of flinty rock, / and from hard stone a remedy for their thirst. / For through the very things by which their enemies were punished, / they themselves received benefit in their need. / For when they were tried, though they were being disciplined in mercy, they learned how the ungodly were tormented when judged in wrath." (Wis 11:4–5, 9)

Reflection: The author of the OT (A) book of Wisdom presents a reflection on the exodus. The Hebrews had suffered in Egypt, but the Lord came to their rescue and, through Moses, led the Israelites out of Egypt. Thus, the Jews have an historical basis for trust in God. The author begins his reflection on the desert wanderings of the Israelites, during which God intervened on behalf of the just. After recalling that God gave them water from the rock, the author notes a pattern he detects in the exodus events: The Israelites were benefited by the very things that punished the Egyptians. The Israelites have their thirst satisfied in the desert by water flowing from the rock, but water punishes the Egyptians—both the water turned to blood and the water that destroyed Pharaoh's army in the Sea of Reeds. Water turned to blood was a plague for the Egyptians, but for the Israelites it was a test—they were disciplined in mercy—to show them how their enemies were punished or chastised. Water in the Sea of Reeds drowned the Egyptian army, but it parted so the Israelites could march through the water to safety.

To be disciplined in mercy means that the Israelites' disobedience did not result in divine condemnation, as did the Egyptians'. The Lord had compassion on his people. He offered forgiveness to them, even though he had power over them. Out of his generosity he eased the distress of their thirst, and out of his kindness he gave them abundant water to drink from a rock. Their thirst, according to the author of Wisdom, is an example of discipline in mercy. Peterson interprets discipline in mercy this way: "You [, O Lord,] put the Israelite spirit to the ultimate test, but your lash tickled them rather than sliced them to ribbons; from it they learned that your friends fared far better than your enemies" (Wis 11:9). NAB states that when the Israelites had been tried, "though only mildly chastised, they recognized how the wicked, condemned in anger, were being tormented" (Wis 11:9).

Thus, Israel's suffering in the desert is interpreted by the author of Wisdom as God's testing, an act of disciplined mercy.

Psalm Response: "Do you think the trainer of nations doesn't correct, / the teacher of Adam doesn't know? / GOD knows, all right— / knows your stupidity, / sees your shallowness. / How blessed the man you train, GOD, / the woman you instruct in your Word." (Ps 94:10–12)

Meditation/Journal: When have you benefited from actions that punished others? When have you been disciplined in mercy? Explain.

Prayer: Happy are the people you discipline with mercy, O LORD, whom you teach your way of life. Do not forsake me, when I fail to understand, but fill me with the grace of insight that I may praise your marvelous works today, tomorrow, and forever. Amen.

Expect Mercy

Scripture: ". . . [I]f you [, O Lord,] punish with such great care and indulgence / the enemies of your servants and those deserving of death, / granting them time and opportunity to give up their wickedness, / with what strictness you have judged your children, / to whose ancestors you gave oaths and covenants full of good promises! / So while chastening us you scourge our enemies ten thousand times more, / so that, when we judge, we may meditate upon your goodness, / and when we are judged, we may expect mercy." (Wis 12:20–22)

Reflection: Verses 19 through 22 of chapter 12 of the OT (A) book of Wisdom, from which the above passage comes, presents a reflection on God's justice. By the way God treats his people's enemies, he teaches his children to temper justice with mercy and to expect mercy from him. According to the author's insight, God punishes with great care the enemies of his people, giving them time to repent. Because the Lord's "immortal spirit is in all things," he "corrects little by little those who trespass," and he "reminds and warns them of the things through which they sin, so that they may be freed from wickedness and put their trust in" him (Wis 12:2). For example, even though God hated the Canaanite practices of sacrificing children and cannibalism (Wis 12:4–7), the all-powerful One spared them and gave them an opportunity to repent (Wis 12:10). Thus, according to the author of Wisdom, by the way God treats his people's enemies, he is teaching his chosen people to temper justice (what is owed) with mercy (generosity). God's people need to learn to be kind, have good hope, and know they can repent (Wis 12:19). In other words, God governs with leniency—moderation—not severity. If he has governed his people strictly, he has also given them oaths and covenants full of good promises (Wis 12:21). When the chastisement of his children is compared to that meted to his children's enemies, their enemies have received more punishment (Wis 12:22). This, according to the author, should teach the Jews that when they judge, they should think about God's goodness, and when they are judged by God, they may expect mercy from him instead of justice.

Peterson accurately captures the meaning of the above passage, writing, "... [Y]ou [, Lord,] judge with clemency; you govern with indulgence, even though you can dump us anytime you want! Your conduct on the judicial bench has taught your people that justice must always be kind; your conduct as a parent has given your children hope in forgiveness. You didn't have to rank reconciliation over sin, but you did. You did indeed castigate the enemies of your people, and they deserved to die, but you gave them plenty of space to repent and change their wicked ways. With your own people you've been both strict and lenient; you gave our forebears all sorts of covenants, assurances, and once-in-a-lifetime deals. For every lash you gave to discipline us, you gave two or three to our enemies. Before we judge others, we should meditate on your goodness; when our turn to be judged comes, we should hope for the same mercy" (Wis 12:20–22). NAB states that God punished his children's enemies with solicitude, indulgence, and measured deliberation, while judging his own people with exactitude. Thus, they should think earnestly about his goodness when they judge and look for mercy when he judges them.

Psalm Response: "Stand up, GOD; pit your holy fury / against my furious enemies. / Wake up, God. My accusers have packed / the courtroom; it's judgment time. / Take your place on the bench, reach for your gavel, / throw out the false charges against me. / I'm ready, confident in your verdict: / 'Innocent.'" (Ps 7:6–8)

Meditation/Journal: In what specific ways has God showed goodness and mercy to you? In what specific ways do you temper justice (what is owed to you) with mercy (generosity)?

Prayer: O Lord, you have taught me to temper justice with mercy. Fill me with your Spirit to guide my meditation on your goodness to me, and direct my thoughts to share the mercy I expect from you with others today, tomorrow, and forever. Amen.

Healing Mercy

Scripture: Lord "your children were not conquered / even by the fangs of venomous serpents, / for your mercy came to their help and healed them. / To remind them of your oracles they were bitten, / and then were quickly delivered, / so that they would not fall into deep forgetfulness / and become unresponsive to your kindness." (Wis 16:10–11)

Reflection: The emphasis of the author of the OT (A) book of Wisdom in chapter 16 is on God's healing of the Israelites (Wis 16:5–14). To make his point, he employs the story found in the HB (OT) book of Numbers (21:5–9) about the serpents that bite the people. The Israelites grumbled against God and Moses in the wilderness, God sent poisonous serpents to bite them, the people repented, Moses asked the LORD to take away the serpents, and God instructed Moses to make a bronze serpent and put it on a pole; anyone bitten needed only to look at the bronze serpent and he or she was healed. The author of Wisdom states that it is not the bronze serpent that healed the Israelites; rather, it was God who healed them. The bronze serpent, according to Wisdom, is "a symbol of deliverance" to remind the Israelites of the law (Wis 16:6b). "For the one who turned toward it was saved, not by the thing that was beheld, but by you, the Savior of all," states the author (Wis 16:7). The author presumes that the Egyptians, the enemies of the Israelites, should have been convinced that it is God who delivers from every evil. The reader must keep in mind that the Egyptians were not in the desert when the Israelites encountered the poisonous serpents! While they were killed by the bites of locusts and flies—plagues—no healing was found for them (Wis 16:9). However, the Israelites were not conquered by the fangs of poisonous serpents, because God's mercy came to their help and healed them. According to the author, this was to keep them from forgetting that it was not any kind of medicine that cured their snake bites, but it was the Lord's word that healed them (Wis 16:12). Only God has power over life and death (Wis 16:13). Only the Lord possesses healing mercy.

Peterson captures the intent of this section of the OT (A) book of Wisdom, writing: Lord, "when your people were plagued by poisonous snakes, . . . it was only a short time before your wrath petered out. In fact, the hardships they endured were more a warning than a punishment, a demonstration that your Law had teeth in it. To remind them of that, you gave them a sign, a bronze serpent, which became a medicine of sorts. To be cured of snakebite all one of our people had to do was face the symbol. Of course, the fake snake didn't do it; you, the Savior of us all, were the Divine Doctor!" (Wis 16:5–9) NAB states, that "when the dire venom of beasts came upon [the Israelites] / and they were dying from the bite of crooked serpents, / your anger [, Lord,] endured not to the end. / But as a warning, for a short time they were terrorized, / though they had a sign of salvation, to remind them of the precept of your law. / For the one who turned toward [the bronze serpent] was saved, / not by what was seen, / but by you, the savior of all" (Wis 16:5–7). Thus, God bestowed healing mercy on his people.

Psalm Response: "GOD, my God, I yelled for help / and you put me together. / GOD, you pulled me out of the grave / gave me another chance at life / when I was down-and-out. / You did it: you changed wild lament / into whirling dance; / You ripped off my black mourning band / and decked me with wildflowers. / I'm about to burst with song; / I can't keep quiet about you. / GOD, my God, / I can't thank you enough." (Ps 30:2–3, 11–12)

Meditation/Journal: In what specific ways have you responded to God's kind, healing mercy? From what has the Divine Doctor healed you? What do you consider to be a sign of salvation?

Prayer: Lord, once your people grumbled against you and Moses, and you sent poisonous snakes to bite them. After they repented, you cured them of snake bite with the sign of your salvation, a bronze serpent on a pole. Be the Divine Doctor to me, and heal me of all that keeps me from praising you today, tomorrow, and forever. Amen.

Wait for Mercy

Scripture: "You who fear the Lord, wait for his mercy; / do not stray, or else you may fall." (Sir 2:7)

Reflection: In the OT (A) book of Jesus son of Sirach—also called Ecclesiasticus or, simply, Sirach—the author—Ben Sira—equates the possession of wisdom with the fear of the Lord. Because the pursuit of wisdom is a common goal across cultures, the fear of the Lord specifies of what Jewish wisdom consists. The fear of the Lord is the beginning of wisdom (Sir 1:14a) states the author; it is both wisdom and discipline (Sir 1:27a). The rewards, blessings, and discipline of wisdom, according to Sirach, are manifested in one's earthly life. Thus, Sirach lists three important teachings (two above and one in the next entry) how the learner is to prepare himself or herself for testing. First, those who fear the Lord—those who seek wisdom—patiently await God's mercy. Peterson states that his mercy is never far away. Patience dictates that people seeking wisdom do not stray, or, according to Peterson, wander off and get lost. The discipline is to stay focused! In other words, serving the Lord faithfully is difficult; it requires any true believer to remain steadfast in the face of trials or distress. However, as Sirach states, those who persevere in the fear of the Lord have never been forsaken (Sir 2:10b).

Second, trust is an essential of biblical faith. Peterson exhorts one to believe in the Lord; one's reward—wisdom—is safe with him. Reliance on God, as demonstrated throughout the Bible, is a discipline that results in wisdom. According to Sirach, the good are always rewarded in this life, even if they go through hard times; when considering generations of the past, no one who trusted in the Lord was ever disappointed (Sir 2:10a). Wisdom (fear of the Lord), an eternal attribute of God, is glory, exultation, gladness, and rejoicing; it delights the heart and gives gladness, joy, and a long life (Sir 1:11–12).

Psalm Response: "Listen, everyone, listen— / earth-dwellers, don't miss this. / All you have / and have-nots, / All together now: listen. / I set plain-spoken wisdom before you, my heart-seasoned understandings of life. / I fine-tuned my ear to the sayings of the wise, / I solve life's riddle with the help of a harp. We aren't immortal. We don't last long." (Ps 49: 1–4, 12a)

Meditation/Journal: When have you waited patiently for the Lord's mercy? Explain. When have you relied upon the Lord? For what? Explain.

Prayer: I wait for your mercy, O Lord; keep me from straying from you. I trust your word. Grant that my fear of you is the beginning of wisdom for me. And grant that throughout my life, I may grow in wisdom by meditating upon all your works today, tomorrow, and forever. Amen.

Hope for Mercy 1

Scripture: "You who fear the Lord, hope for good things, / for lasting joy and mercy. For the Lord is compassionate and merciful, / he forgives sins and saves in time of distress." (Sir 2:9, 11)

Reflection: The third of three things Sirach teaches about wisdom (the fear of the Lord) is hope. In the OT (A) book of Jesus son of Sirach—also called Ecclesiasticus or, simply, Sirach—the author—Ben Sira—equates the possession of wisdom with the fear of the Lord. Because the pursuit of wisdom is a common goal across cultures, the fear of the Lord specifies of what Jewish wisdom consists. "To fear the Lord is the beginning of wisdom" (Sir 1:14a) states the author; it "is wisdom and discipline" (Sir 1:27a). The rewards, blessings, and discipline of wisdom, according to Sirach, are manifested in one's earthly life. Thus, Sirach lists three important teachings (two in the above entry and one in this entry) how the learner is to prepare himself or herself for testing. Sirach asks, ". . . [H]as anyone called upon [the Lord] and been neglected?" (Sir 2:10c) The reader must answer that no one who fears the Lord and hopes for good things, for lasting joy and mercy, has not received God's care. The lasting joy and mercy are for happiness in this life, not life hereafter.

Peterson states this teaching, writing: "Fear the Lord, but look on the bright side; there'll be blessings and mercies galore" (Sir 2:9). If the reader looks through biblical history, he or she will notice that some people "were hopefully infused; others . . . were hopelessly confused," states Peterson (Sir 2:11). He adds, "You who fear the Lord, love him. He'll light your candles" (Sir 2:9). While waiting and trust (previous entry) with hope (this entry) are three expressions of the right attitude of those who desire wisdom, verse 11 above echoes Exodus 34:6 ("The LORD, the LORD, / a God merciful and gracious, / slow to anger, / and abounding in steadfast love and faithfulness, / keeping steadfast love for the thousandth generation, / forgiving iniquity and transgression and sin . . . ."), a statement about God's character. Those who wait, trust, and hope in fear of the Lord discover, like those in the past, that the Lord understands the suffering of his creation, shows mercy to those seeking wisdom, offers forgiveness, and saves them. No one who has called upon the Lord in hope has ever been neglected, according to Sirach.

Psalm Response: "Watch this: God's eye is on those who respect him, / the ones who are looking for his love. / He's ready to come to their rescue in bad times; / in lean times he keeps body and soul together. / We're depending on GOD; / he's everything we need. / What's more, our hearts brim with joy / since we've taken for our own his holy name." (Ps 33:18–21)

Meditation/Journal: What role does hope play in your search for wisdom? In what specific ways have you experienced your hope for mercy fulfilled by God?

Prayer: I hope for good things from you, O Lord; I seek lasting joy and mercy. Out of your compassion, grace me with happiness and kindness. Fill me with your wisdom, and grant that I may trust you and serve you all the days of my life. Amen.

Majestic Mercy

Scripture: "Those who fear the Lord do not disobey his words, / and those who love him keep his ways. / Those who fear the Lord seek to please him, / and those who love him are filled with his law. / Those who fear the Lord prepare their hearts, / and humble themselves before him. / Let us fall into the hands of the Lord, / but not into the hands of mortals; / for equal to his majesty is his mercy, / and equal to his name are his works." (Sir 2:15–18)

Reflection: The author of the OT (A) book of Sirach characterizes those who seek wisdom, those who fear the Lord. First, he states that God-fearers, wisdom-seekers, are those who love the Lord. For Ben Sira, the fear of the Lord and the love of the Lord are the same. Second, those who fear (love) the Lord keep his words and follow his law (Torah), his ways, his lifestyle. The author is not thinking about a code of external observance, but as a constant and effective desire to find the will of God and to act on it (wisdom), to please the Lord. Thus, those who seek wisdom (fear God) humble themselves before him, like people of a kingdom kneel or bow before their king. That prepares for the final verse about falling into the hands of the Lord. Usually, the phrase connotes a calamity leading to destruction or even death, but Ben Sira transforms it into an image of rescue and salvation. He understands the hands of the Lord to be God's instruments of mercy. Like the majesty showed by the people of a kingdom to their king, Sirah declares that the Lord's mercy is equal to his majesty; God displays majestic mercy. His covenant love showed to those seeking wisdom is beyond equal to his majesty. Also, equal to the importance of his name are his works. In other words, falling into God's hands is safe, because those who do so receive majestic mercy.

Peterson captures the tone of the above verses this way: "Those who fear the Lord hear his word. Those who love him keep the highway in good repair. Those who fear the Lord find out what he likes. Those who love him enjoy his teachings. Those who fear the Lord prepare their hearts and humble their souls in his presence. Those who fear the Lord follow his life-maps; they don't care when the Final Inspection will come. . . . The Lord is great . . . . But then, of course, there's always his forgiveness" (Sir 2:18–23).

Psalm Response: "I lift you high in praise, my God, O my King! / and I'll bless you name into eternity. / GOD is magnificent; he can never be praised enough. / There are no boundaries to his greatness. / Generation after generation stands in awe of your work [, O God]; / each one tells stories of your mighty acts. / Your marvelous doings are headline news; / I could write a book full of the details of your greatness. / The fame of your goodness spreads across the country; / your righteousness is on everyone's lips. / GOD is all mercy and grace— / not quick to anger, is rich in love." (Ps 145:1, 3–4, 6–8)

Meditation/Journal: What majestic mercy and wisdom have you discovered in the Lord's words? When did you most recently fall into the hands of the Lord? Explain. What majestic mercy did you receive?

Prayer: I come before you in prayer, O Lord, eager to listen to your words in order to follow your ways. With your abundant love catch me when I fall into your hands. See me standing humbly before you, and prepare my heart to receive your majestic mercy. Hear my prayer today, tomorrow, and forever. Amen.

Great Mercy 2

Scripture: "Do not say, 'I sinned, yet what has happened to me?' / for the Lord is slow to anger. / Do not be so confident of forgiveness / that you add sin to sin. / Do not say, 'His mercy is great, he will forgive the multitude of my sins,' / for both mercy and wrath are with him, / and his anger will rest on sinners." (Sir 5:4–6)

Apocrypha/Deuterocanonicals

Reflection: Beginning with chapter 5, Sirach presents three topics of central importance throughout the OT (A) book. The first one, wealth, is addressed in this way: "Do not rely on your wealth," advises the author, or say, 'I have enough'" (Sir 5:1). Peterson gets at the meaning of this negative precept by stating, "Don't rely on your assets. Don't say, 'I have enough to live comfortably for the rest of my life'" (Sir 5:1). It is important not to rely on wealth. because one who seeks wisdom relies upon God. Likewise, Sirach advises, "Do not say, 'Who can have power over me?' / for the Lord will surely punish you" (Sir 5:3). Those who seek wisdom know that God has power over all. Peterson captures this idea, writing, "Don' say, 'I'm not a pushover for anybody' or 'Who'll topple me from my pedestal?' Why? Because a vindictive God will knock your block off" (Sir 5:3). Those two negative precepts prepare for the next three found in the passage above.

These three deal with presumption based on wealth. First, "Don't say, 'I've sinned and I'm already forgiven!'" says Peterson. That is presumption. "The Most High will reward your confession when he's good and ready" (Sir 5:4). Second, "Don't be over-confident about forgiveness, and for sure don't commit another sin just because you can," states Peterson (Sir 5:5). That is presumption. And third, "Don't say, 'The Lord's capacity for forgiveness is great, more than enough to forgive my own sins.' Why? Because the Lord can deliver his wrath quickly, while sinners are notoriously slow-moving targets" (Sir 5:6). That, too, is presumption. Those who rely upon their wealth also rely upon their presumption of God's great mercy. According to Sirach, to presume mercy is to invite disaster. In other words, the reader should be cautious of beliefs, which may seem extremely reasonable, but have no actual evidence. While it is true that God's mercy is great, it cannot be presumed, nor can God be manipulated into giving it. Along with presumption, pride, false security, and impenitence cannot escape God's wrath. Wealth should not be gained by thievery (Sir 5:8, 14).

Psalm Response: "I set plainspoken wisdom before you, / my heart-seasoned understandings of life. / I fine-tuned my ear to the sayings of the wise, / I solve life's riddle with the help of a harp. / So why should I fear in bad times, / hemmed in by enemy malice, / Shoved around by bullies, / demeaned by the arrogant rich? / Anyone can see that the brightest and best die, / wiped out right along with fools and dunces. / So don't be impressed with those who get rich / and pile up fame and fortune. / They can't take it with them; / fame and fortune all get left behind." (Ps 49:3–6, 10, 16–17a)

Meditation/Journal: Upon what or whom do you rely? Explain. What are three of your presumptions about wealth? How do they affect your trust in the Lord's great mercy?

Prayer: O Lord, protect me from presuming that I will receive your great mercy for forgiveness. Rather, instill within me a greater appreciation for your love and the gifts you bestow upon me. Fill me with the wisdom to use your gifts wisely today, tomorrow, and forever. Amen.

Mercy and Wrath

Scripture: "In an assembly of sinners a fire is kindled, / and in a disobedient nation wrath blazes up. / [The Lord] did not spare the neighbors of Lot, whom he loathed on account of their arrogance. / Even if there were only one stiff-necked person, / it would be a wonder if he remained unpunished. / For mercy and wrath are with the Lord, / he is mighty to forgive—but he also pours out wrath." (Sir 16:6, 8, 11)

Reflection: Biblical divine wrath is not a concept upon which modern people desire to meditate. Biblical wrath refers to retributive justice towards persons or nations whose actions God judges to deserve some form of condemnation. In chapter 16 of the OT (A) book of Sirach, Ben Sira notes God's biblical wrath in response to the rebellion of Korah (Sir 16:6; Num 11:1–3). He also mentions the destruction of Sodom (Sir 16:8; Gen 19:1–38). The above passage lists only two of the examples Ben Sira gives to illustrate divine wrath. He concludes his reflection on God's capacity to punish sinners by stating that if only one stiff-necked person survived, it would be surprising, as expressed by Peterson. In other words, no stiff-necked person is spared divine wrath, according to Sirach.

The opposite of divine wrath is divine mercy; as Ben Sira makes clear, both wrath and mercy come from the Lord; they exist side by side in God. While he at time displays wrath (NAB says anger), he, also at times, forgives (NAB says he remits and forgives). Peterson captures the meaning of this passage, writing, "Mercy and anger are both on God's side; mercy upholding, sustaining; anger flooding, overflowing" (Sir 16:12). It is important to note that both wrath and mercy are human emotions attributed to God anthropomorphically—God is pictured having a human form (usually as an old man) with human attributes (wrath and mercy). In other words, biblical writers imagined God as looking like themselves and possessing the same emotions (wrath, mercy, love, etc.) that they experienced themselves having.

Psalm Response: "[The Israelites] gave witness that God was their rock, / that High God was their redeemer, / But they didn't mean a word of it; / they lied through their teeth the whole time. / They could not have cared less about him, / wanting nothing to do with his Covenant. / And God? Compassionate! / Forgave the sin! Didn't destroy! / Over and over he reined in his anger, / restrained his considerable wrath. / He knew what they were made of; / he knew there wasn't much to them . . . ." (Ps 78:35–39)

Meditation/Journal: What are your thoughts on divine wrath and divine mercy? After reflecting on how wrath and mercy co-exist in God, according to Sirach, what do you conclude?

Prayer: Most High God of wrath and mercy, when you judged it necessary, you dispersed retributive justice to those whose actions deserved punishment, but your anger was always tempered with your merciful forgiveness. Keep your wrath in check when you judge me by bestowing your mercy on me today, tomorrow, and forever. Amen.

Great Mercy 3

Scripture: "Great as is [the Lord's] mercy, so also is his chastisement; / he judges a person according to his or her deeds." (Sir 16:12)

Reflection: Biblical scholars note that the author—Ben Sira—of the OT (A) book of Sirach addresses the issue of collective mercy and punishment versus individual mercy and punishment, but he does not resolve the issue (Sir 16:5–23). In other words, the author reflects upon the biblical record of collective mercy and punishment showed to the whole community of Israel, when it is only a single individual or subcommunity that has sinned or received mercy. That is why the verse in the above passage states that while the Lord's mercy is great, so also is his chastisement. Peterson says, "[The Lord's] mercy is mammoth; he adjusts it to fit the situation, judging human beings by what they do and not what they say" (Sir 16:12). According to Ben Sira, the Lord judges a person according to his or her deeds. While the previous biblical understanding that God judges the community by the deeds of a person is not removed, Ben Sira emphasizes that the Lord judges the individual according to his or her deeds as deserving great mercy or punishment.

Then, to support his reflection that it is the individual who is the direct recipient of God's great mercy or punishment, he states, according to Peterson, "Sinners won't get far with their plunder; the purveyor of justice won't be embarrassed in the end" (Sir 16:13). God, who judges justly, rewards those who patiently persist in doing good deeds. NAB states that criminals do not escape with their plunder, while God fulfills the hope of the righteous. Then, to emphasize his point, as will be seen in the next entry, Ben Sira declares that God rewards with great mercy those who do good deeds, just like he punishes those who do evil deeds.

Psalm Response: "Don't bother your head with braggarts / or wish you could succeed like the wicked. / In no time they'll shrivel like grass clippings / and wilt like cut flowers in the sun. / Get insurance with GOD and do a good deed, / settle down and stick to [it]. / Keep company with GOD, / get in on the best. Open up before GOD, keep nothing back; / he'll do whatever needs to be done . . . ." (Ps 37:1–5)

Meditation/Journal: If God were to judge you today according to your deeds, would you receive great mercy or chastisement? Why?

Prayer: While you are great in mercy, O Lord, you are also great in punishment. Send your Holy Spirit to inspire and guide me to do good deeds all my life. Make me a recipient of your great mercy today, tomorrow, and forever. Amen.

Great Mercy 4

Scripture: "[The Lord] makes room for every act of mercy; / everyone receives in accordance with his or her deeds. / Lo, heaven and the highest heaven, / the abyss and the earth, tremble at his visitation!" (Sir 16:14, 18)

Reflection: In the OT (A) book of Sirach, Ben Sira, the author, continues the reflection begun in the previous entry by stating, according to Peterson, "There'll be a reward for every merciful act done; all will get precisely what they deserve and what makes sense given our shared earthly pilgrimage" (Sir 16:14). Then, Peterson includes verses 15 and 16, which appear in some ancient manuscripts but not in all Bibles, and reflects the author's interpretation of the events preceding the exodus: "The Lord dimmed the heart of Pharaoh lest he dazzle him with his powerful works. The Lord's mercy is apparent to all worldly creatures. He separated the light from the dark for his children" (Sir 15:15–16). In other words, the narrative about God separating light from darkness (Gen 1:4) is understood by Ben Sira as an act of the Lord's mercy for the Hebrews, just like the darkening of Pharaoh's heart is an act of the Lord's punishment for the Egyptians.

Ben Sira cautions the reader not to tell himself or herself that the Lord cannot see him or her, that he or she is just another person among billions of people inhabiting the third planet from the sun. To the God who created the heavens, the earth, and the underworld, the God who exists in past, present, and future, no one is hidden. Indeed, when the Lord looks at the three-storied earth—heaven, earth, underworld—the foundations quiver and quake. What the human mind cannot grasp or comprehend or make sense of is the fact, according to Sirach, that no one's deeds escape God's notice for a reward of great mercy or punishment.

Psalm Response: "Keep company with GOD, / get in on the best. / Before you know it, the wicked will have had it; / you'll stare at his once famous place and—nothing! / Down-to-earth people will move in and take over, / relishing a huge bonanza. / Bad guys have it in for the good guys, / obsessed with doing them in. / But God isn't losing any sleep; to him / they're a joke with no punch line." (Ps 37:4, 10–13)

Meditation/Journal: What reward of great divine mercy have you recently received for a good deed you did? Explain.

Prayer: Lord, fill me with the wisdom of understanding your ways. Do not let me become a senseless and misguided person, but make me one who does good deeds and receives your great mercy. I stand before you and place my trust in your great mercy today, tomorrow, and forever. Amen.

Great Mercy 5

Scripture: "Return to the Most High and turn away from iniquity, / and hate intensely what he abhors. / Who will sing praises to the Most High in Hades / in place of the living who give thanks? / From the dead, as from one who does not exist, thanksgiving has ceased; / those who are alive and well sing the Lord's praises. / How great is the mercy of the Lord, / and his forgiveness for those who return to him!" (Sir 17:26–29)

Reflection: In chapter 17 of the OT (A) book of Sirach, Ben Sira, the author, begins his reflection by calling to mind that human beings were created by God out of the earth, and to the earth they return as dust (Sir 17:1). The story of the creation of human beings launches Ben Sira's thoughts about God putting the fear of the Lord (wisdom) into all living beings (Sir 17:4, 8) and filling them with knowledge and understanding and teaching them the difference between good and evil (Sir 17:7). From the creation of people, Ben Sira quickly moves to the creation of the people of Israel (Sir 17:12–23). The role of wise people is to praise God's holy name and to proclaim the grandeur of his works (Sir 17:9–10). Because people's sins are not hidden from God (Sir 17:20), his great mercy is showed when they repent and return to him; he encourages those who lose hope (Sir 17:24). Thus, Ben Sira summons his readers: "Turn back to the Lord and forsake your sins; / pray in his presence and lessen your offense" (Sir 17:25).

Repentance glorifies the Lord, because it demonstrates that the person repenting hates what God hates. If a person needs a reason to repent in the present, Ben Sira states that it is available only to the living. Life consists in praise of God. No one can sing praises to the Most High in Hades (the Geek name for the underworld; the Hebrew name for the underworld is Sheol, as in NAB). Once a person is dead, it is like he or she never existed; thanksgiving to God has ceased. Those who live and are well sing the Lord's praise. Thus, those who receive God's forgiveness by returning to him experience his great mercy in this life. Peterson captures the meaning of this passage, exhorting: "Don't give up as you wait in line for the final disposition and prayer. Can those in the grave praise the Most High? Which of the dead can pray better than the living, at least the ones who believe in God? . . . Repent before death comes; after death, repentance is too late. Confess your sins while you're living; confess while you still have your wits about you. Praise God, and you'll glory in his commiseration. How massive is the mercy of God! How great is the compassion of the Lord!" (Sir 17:26–29) Repentance, returning to the Most High, in this life gives a human being the experience of God's great or massive mercy.

Psalm Response: "Unbutton my lips, dear God; / I'll let loose with your praise. / Going through the motions doesn't please you, / a flawless performance is nothing to you. / I learned God-worship / when my pride was shattered. / Heart-shattered lives ready for love / don't for a moment escape God's notice." (Ps 51:15–17)

Meditation/Journal: From what do you need to repent (to return to the Most High)? What experience of returning to the Most High in your past was one of experiencing the great (massive) mercy of God? Explain.

Prayer: Your scribe, Ben Sira, calls me to return to you, Most High. Fill me with your grace that I may repent now and praise and thank you. I know your forgiveness is unmeasurable, and I desire to experience the greatness of your mercy today, tomorrow, and forever. Amen.

Poured Mercy

Scripture: "He who lives forever created the whole universe; / the Lord alone is just. / When human beings have finished, they are just beginning, / and when they stop, they are still perplexed. / That is why the Lord is patient with them / and pours out his mercy upon them. / . . . [T]he compassion of the Lord is for every living thing. (Sir 18:1–2, 7, 11, 13b)

Reflection: The poem that initiates chapter 18 of the OT (A) book of Sirach (18:1–14) begins by expressing the unsurpassed majesty of God and contrasts it with the puny stature of human beings. It resolves the chasm between God and people by stressing God's compassion for humans. The author of Sirach, Ben Sira, marvels at God's power: He is eternal; he is the creator (Sir 18:1); and his majesty cannot be measured and his mercies cannot be counted (Sir 18:5–6). Peterson states, "The one who lives in time-without-time created everything in one fell swoop. Who could tell the story of these eternal happenings . . . ? . . . Who could inventory the total creativity of God? God alone . . . will remain King in time-without-time!" (Sir 18:1, 4–5). The insignificance of human beings, according to Ben Sira, is demonstrated in their cyclical perplexity (Sir 18:7) and in their short lifetimes (Sir 16:9–10). "[M]ere drops in the sea," are human beings, states Peterson, "mere grains on the beach, when compared to time-without-time" (Sir 18:10).

Because humans are incapable of appreciating God's divine majesty and glory manifested in creation, God is patient with them to the point of pouring his mercy upon them. Peterson states, "Because of the time differential, God is patient with humans; he showers his mercy upon them" (Sir

18:11). Indeed, the Lord has compassion on all living things. "He recognizes their imperfection because it sticks out," writes Peterson (Sir 18:12). "So what's lacking he quickly resupplies; he restores them to a state of grace" (Sir 18:12). Those who accept God's discipline, who are eager for wisdom, receive his poured mercy. "He's pleased when those who learn the ins and outs of mercy put them to work right away," states Peterson (Sir 18:14).

Psalm Response: "God's love is meteoric, / his loyalty astronomic, / His purpose titanic, / his verdicts oceanic. / Yet in his largeness / nothing gets lost; / Not a man, not a mouse, / slips through the cracks. / How exquisite your love, O God! / How eager we are to run under your wings." (Ps 36:5–7)

Meditation/Journal: In what specific ways has being a human being made you the recipient of God's poured-out mercy? What was your response?

Prayer: Lord, I am not able to plumb the depth of your divinity, because my limitations are human. I ask for your patience. I ask you to pour your mercy upon me. Fill me with your wisdom, and make me eager to receive your compassion today, tomorrow, and forever. Amen.

No Mercy 5

Scripture: "Forgive your neighbor the wrong he has done, / and then your sins will be pardoned when you pray. / Does anyone harbor anger against another, / and expect healing from the Lord? / If one has no mercy toward another like himself, / can he then seek pardon for his own sins? (Sir 28:2–4)

Reflection: In chapter 28 of the OT (A) book of Sirach, the author presents his reflections on forgiveness. "Anger and wrath," he writes, "these also are abominations, / yet a sinner holds on to them" (Sir 27:30). From the perspective of wisdom, anger and wrath belong to God. Furthermore, anger and wrath punish the person letting them fester within him or her. Peterson says, "Anger and furor are both detestable, yet the sinner holds on to them for dear life" (Sir 27:30). The danger, as Peterson puts it, is this: "If you seek revenge upon another, you'll get your comeuppance from the Lord; the Lord already has you on the Revenge Watch List" (Sir 28:1). The individual full of wisdom knows that forgiveness begets forgiveness; mercy begets mercy. "Forgive you neighbors on the near side when they sin against you," writes Peterson; "in return, your neighbors on the far side will do the same" (Sir 28:2). What is true about forgiving one's neighbor and being forgiven is also true of one's relationship with God. Again, Peterson catches the importance of this wisdom, writing, "Should anyone harbor anger against another and expect to be forgiven?" (Sir 28:3). The answer the reader must give is, of course, No. "If you don't show mercy toward another, should the Lord still show mercy to you?" (Sir 28:4). And, again, the reader must answer No.

The standard of forgiveness proposed to those who seek wisdom by Ben Sira echoes the standard proposed by Jesus in the CB (NT). The Markan Jesus tells his disciples, "Whenever you stand praying, forgive, if you have anything against anyone; so that your Father in heaven may also forgive you your trespasses" (Mark 11:25). The Matthean Jesus teaches his disciples to pray, saying, "Our Father in heaven, / . . . forgive us our debts, / as we also have forgiven our debtors (Matt 6:9b, 12). Then he adds, "For if you forgive others their trespasses, you heavenly Father will also forgive you; but if you do not forgive others, neither will your Father forgive your trespasses" (Matt 6:14–15; 18:32–35; Jas 2:13). The person seeking wisdom (fear of the Lord), according to Ben Sira and Jesus cannot expect to receive mercy (forgiveness) from God without also granting mercy (forgiveness) to fellow human beings. No mercy showed to others by a person results in no mercy showed by God to that person!

Psalm Response: "Count yourself lucky, how happy you must be— / you get a fresh start, / your slate's wiped clean. / Count yourself lucky— / GOD holds nothing against you / and you're holding nothing back from him." (Ps 32:1–2)

Meditation/Journal: What has been your latest experience of forgiving? To whom did you show mercy? What has been your latest experience of not forgiving? To whom did you not show mercy? Which experience brought you closer to another and to God? Explain.

Prayer: God, you have taught me through Ben Sira and Jesus of Nazareth that if I want to be forgiven by you, I must forgive those who offend me. Grant me the grace to show mercy to those who wrong me that I may display to others the merciful pardon you extend to me today, tomorrow, and forever. Amen.

Rejoice in Mercy

Scripture: "... [T]he Lord will listen to the prayer of one who is wronged. / The one whose service is pleasing to the Lord will be accepted, / and his prayer will reach to the clouds. / The prayer of the humble pierces the clouds, / and it will not rest until it reaches its goal; / it will not desist until the Most High responds / and does justice for the righteous, and executes judgment. / Indeed, the Lord will not delay . . . until he judges the case of his people / and makes them rejoice in his mercy." (Sir 35:16, 20–22a, 25)

Reflection: According to Ben Sira, the author of the OT (A) book of Sirach, the person who pursues wisdom knows the power of prayer. According to Ben Sira, the prayer of anyone who is wronged is heard by God. According to Peterson, "The prayers of those who adore God will be warmly welcomed; their humble prayers will reach the clouds" (Sir 35:29). It is important to note that the author has in mind a three-storied universe; while people live on the flat, plate-like surface of the earth, a dome stretches over the earth, and above the dome, in which there are clouds, lives God. That is why Ben Sira conceives of prayer as rising from the earth, where people live, to the clouds, above which is where God lives. According to Peterson, the prayers of God-adorers "must arrive before they can be acted upon, but they won't be discarded before they're reviewed" by God. "The Most High will take the proper action, if any is needed; he'll get to it as soon as possible" (Sir 35:21). Peterson adds that the Most High God "will render the judgment of judgments [on his faithful people for doing their part] and shower them with mercy" (Sir 35:25).

Not only does Ben Sira teach the surety of God's hearing of prayer, but he also teaches the surety of God's mercy. The wise person knows that his or her prayers ascend to God like smoke rises from incense burned on charcoal. And the God who lives above the dome of the sky listens to what his people say to him. He answers their prayers, and they rejoice in the mercy he shows them in so doing. Believing that God hears and answers is enough for those who reverence God to rejoice in his mercy. Those who seek wisdom, which comes from the Lord and remains with a person forever (Sir 1:1), rejoice in God's mercy.

Psalm Response: "Have mercy on us, God of all; look kindly upon us and show us the light of your compassion. [The Gentile nations] will see the holy things you've done for us, just as we'll see the holy things you've done for them. They'll come to know what we know now: There's no God but you, Lord. Create new signage; do new wonders. Gather together all the tribes of Jacob." (Sir 36:1, 4-6, 13)

Meditation/Journal: What do you understand prayer to be? When was your prayer answered and you rejoiced in God's mercy? Explain. What did that experience teach you (give you wisdom) about the power of prayer? How does the modern solar-centered cosmology affect Ben Sira's understanding and description of prayer? Explain.

Prayer: Most High God, when I pray to you for help or praise you in thanksgiving for answering my prayer, I trust that you will do what is best for me. Fill me with your Holy Spirit, and inspire me to seek only what is pleasing to you. I rejoice in your mercy today, tomorrow, and forever. Amen.

Welcomed Mercy

Scripture: "[The Lord's] mercy is as welcome in time of distress / as clouds of rain in time of drought." (Sir 35:26)

Reflection: Ben Sira, the author of the OT (A) book of Sirach, concludes his reflection on prayer with the above verse. Peterson translates that verse to read: "In the time of great trouble, [the Lord's] mercy will come like clouds of rain in a time of drought" (Sir 35:26). In other words, just as people welcome rain clouds at a time of drought, people suffering distress welcome God's mercy. The distress mentioned in the above verse refers to the foreign domination of the Seleucid dynasty, the rulers of Syria and its surrounding areas after the breakup of the Greek empire of Alexander the Great, following his death (356-326 BCE).

The prayer that follows the verse above (Sir 36:1-22) is a lament that reflects a political perspective. In the prayer, Ben Sira asks God to show mercy, while putting all the nations in fear of him (Sir 36:1). "Lift up your hand against foreign nations / and let them see your might," states Ben Sira in the prayer (Sir 36:2). The prayer continues: "Crush the heads of hostile rulers / who say, 'There is no one but ourselves' / Gather all the tribes of Jacob, and give them their inheritance as at the beginning" (Sir 36:12-13, 16). In other words, Ben Sira calls for the reestablishment of Israel as a nation distinct from other nations so that Israel in general and Jerusalem in particular can be restored to glory (see the Psalm Response for more of

Ben Sira's prayer). Ben Sira prays that God will save his people again, just like he did when they were slaves in Egypt (Sir 36:6–7). God's mercy is welcomed at this time of distress, according to Ben Sira, just like rain clouds are welcomed at a time of drought.

Psalm Response: "Have mercy upon your people, [, Lord,] who invoke your name; upon the house of Israel, whom you've named your firstborn. Have mercy on the city you have made holy, Jerusalem, a residential place of peace and quiet. Fill Zion with your majesty and the Temple with glory. Reward those who've kept their faith intact; may they find your word still relevant. Hear the prayers of your servants; be gracious to us . . . ." (Sir 36:17–19, 21–22a)

Meditation/Journal: When have you welcomed divine mercy like rain clouds during a drought? What distress were you in? For what did you pray? What mercy did you receive from God?

Prayer: When I am in distress, I lift up my voice to you, O Lord, and, invoking your name, I seek your mercy. I wait for you to hear my prayer, as one awaits rain during a drought. Your mercy will declare that you are the Lord, the God of the ages today, tomorrow, and forever. Amen.

Mercy not Given Up

Scripture: "Solomon reigned in an age of peace, / because God made all his borders tranquil. / How wise you were when you were young. / You stained your honor, and defiled your family line . . . . But the Lord will never give up his mercy, / or cause any of his works to perish; / he will never blot out the descendants of his chosen ones, / or destroy the family line of him who loved him." (Sir 47:13–14a, 20, 22ab)

Reflection: The above passage comes from the section of Sirach that is known as the praise of the heroes or the honor of the ancestors, "famous men" (literally, *hesed* [mercy] men; Sir 44:1), that begins at 44:1 and ends at 51:24. In Ben Sira's praise of Israel's heroes—all known in earlier biblical literature—the author recalls the legacy of men (no women are included in the list) to illustrate what it means to be honored for their attainment of wisdom. In chapter 47, from which the above Scripture passage is taken, Ben Sira praises Solomon, King David's son. Peterson states that Solomon was "renowned for his wise decisions" and "[b]ecause of him, people were able to live in security. His rule was marked by peace" (Sir 47:13–14). Even though Solomon is known throughout biblical history as being wise, he stained his honor by adding foreign women to his harem; those women brought their foreign gods with them. Ultimately, upon Solomon's death, his kingdom split between what became known as the Kingdom of Israel in the north (ten tribes) and the Kingdom of Judah in the south (two tribes). In the north, kingship was determined by who defeated (killed) the reigning king. In the south, kingship was determined by continuing the line of David. Peterson puts it this way: "The Lord didn't mess with Solomon's mind or take away his wisdom; he didn't expel his children from the line of David or bring it to an end. So Solomon dedicated what was left of his kingdom to the memory of Jacob and kept it in the Davidic line" (Sir 47:22–23). In this section of the book, Ben Sira presents the unfaithfulness of King Solomon to the covenant, while also presenting the faithfulness of the Lord to the covenant. The point is that the line of David would never be destroyed; it is often referred to as the everlasting covenant. Through the prophet Nathan, God speaks to David, saying, "Your house and your kingdom shall be made sure forever before me; your throne shall be established forever" (2 Sam 7:16; 1 Kgs 11:13, 38–39). This Jewish belief that God made an eternal covenant with David becomes a messianic expectation after the last kings of Judah die in Babylonian Captivity with no known heirs. Thus, the wisdom for which Solomon was renowned is remembered and praised by Ben Sira, but the mercy of the Lord is more renowned than even Solomon's wisdom.

Psalm Response: "A long time ago you [, Holy God of Israel, our King,] spoke in a vision, / you spoke to your faithful beloved: / 'I've crowned a hero, / I chose the best I could find, / I found David, my servant, / poured holy oil on his head, / And I'll keep my hand steadily on him, / yes, I'll stick with him through thick and thin. / Yes, I'm setting him apart as the First of the royal line, / High King over all of earth's kings. / I'll preserve him eternally in my love, / I'll faithfully do all I so solemnly promised. / I'll guarantee his family tree / and underwrite his rule.'" (Ps 89:19–21, 27–29)

Meditation/Journal: Which of your ancestors was known for his or her wisdom? Explain. In what specific way was God's mercy manifested in his or her life?

Prayer: Lord, in the past you filled rulers, prophets, and teachers with your wisdom as demonstrations of your mercy. Help me to learn your wisdom from them that I may become an instrument of your steadfast love to others today, tomorrow, and forever. Amen.

Prayer for Mercy 2

Scripture: "Hear, O Lord, our prayer and our supplication, and for your own sake deliver us, and grant us favor in the sight of those who have carried us into exile; so that all the earth may know that you are the Lord our God, for Israel and his descendants are called by your name. For it is not because of any righteous deeds of our ancestors or our kings that we bring before you our prayer for mercy, O Lord our God." (Bar 2:14–15, 19)

Reflection: The book of the prophet Baruch is considered part of the OT (A) by Protestants. However, it is considered part of the HB (OT) by Catholics, and, as such, is placed in Bibles after Jeremiah and Lamentations, because Baruch is mentioned as Jeremiah's secretary in the book of the prophet Jeremiah (32:12–13, 16; 36:4–5, 8, 10, 13–19, 26–27, 32; 43:3, 6; 45:1–2). The passage above is taken from the second of four major parts of the book of Baruch; it is known as the penitential prayer (Bar 1:15–3:8). While the prayer resembles one found in Daniel 9:4–19, it was not composed until the second or first century BCE, even though it reflects the exile of the Jews in Babylon. Basically, the purpose of the prayer is to show that penitence is the means for Jews to move from the sinfulness of the past to the obedience and praise of the restored community in Jerusalem.

The unknown author of the prayer begs the Lord to deliver the exiles and, in so doing, to grant them favor in the sight of their captors that the whole earth will know the Lord, the God of Israel, and his descendants who are known by his name. By saving Israel for his own sake, the Lord enables Israel to praise him! The demise of Israel will become a source of embarrassment for the Lord. Israel is possessed and protected by God; if Israel perishes in exile, God's nation will not be able to praise him. The prayer is a petition for the Lord's mercy; Israel did not heed the prophet Jeremiah's pro-Babylonian policy (Jer 27:12–13). Peterson captures the tone of this section of the prayer: "We've turned away from you [, Lord God,], yes, but look at it from our enemies' point of view. They think you turned away from us. We pray that you prove them wrong by granting us the favor of your presence again. All the world would then know that you're our God'; your name will be invoked wherever the house of Israel is dispersed" (Bar 2:14–15). Then, later, he adds: "Our prayers aren't based on the just deeds of our ancestors or our kings; our prayers are our own. We bow before you today. Give us another chance!" (Bar 2:19).

Psalm Response: "All-powerful Lord, God of Israel, the stressful soul and the anxious spirit cry out to you non-stop. Hear us, O Lord. You've got the vantage point of eternity from which to judge things, but we feel we are failing miserably and need your mercy. Our ancestors sinned in your sight and died the slow death; they didn't listen to your voice and their evil deeds have left a mark on us. So please look beyond the sins of our forebears and remember who you are and how highly we think of you now. You're our Lord God; we praised you once; we will praise you again." (Bar 3:1–6)

Medication/Journal: When did you last pray for mercy? What was the occasion? How was your prayer answered? Write a penitential prayer using the above Reflection and/or Psalm Response as a model.

Prayer: Hear, O Lord, my prayer for mercy. I declare your glory and your righteousness, and I acknowledge my own sinfulness for failing to listen to your voice. Please deal with me out of your kindness and great compassion today, tomorrow, and forever. Amen.

Hope for Mercy 2

Scripture: "... I have put my hope in the Everlasting to save you, / and joy has come to me from the Holy One, / because of the mercy that will soon come to you / from your everlasting savior." (Bar 4:22)

Reflection: As already noted in the entry above, the book of the prophet Baruch is considered part of the OT (A) by Protestants. However, it is considered part of the HB (OT) by Catholics, and, as such, is placed in Bibles after Jeremiah and Lamentations, because Baruch is mentioned as Jeremiah's secretary in the book of the prophet Jeremiah (32:12–13, 16; 36:4–5, 8, 10, 13–19, 26–27, 32; 43:3, 6; 45:1–2). The passage above is taken from the fourth of four major parts of the book of Baruch; it is known as the Zion poem (Bar 4:5–5:9). The Zion poem has been influenced by Isaiah 40–66 and Deuteronomy 28–32. The basic idea expressed in the poem is that the

Jews of the exile looked back on the sin of their ancestors and, through penitence, could look forward to a return to God. It is called the Zion poem, because Jerusalem is personified as a grieving widow (Bar 4:9–29). In a subsection of the poem, Jerusalem addresses the Diaspora (Bar 4:17–29); the Diaspora is the area outside Jerusalem, called "the neighbors of Zion" (Bar 4:14). It is from that personification that the above verses come.

The poem presumes that Jerusalem's children are in exile; they are in the country of their enemy. Jerusalem exhorts them to cry to the Lord, the Everlasting, in whom Jerusalem has put her hope for salvation, from whom has come joy because of the imminent mercy from the everlasting savior. Peterson's translation captures the poetic hope for mercy that is contained in the poem: "Have faith, my children; you too should call to God. He'll rescue you from the hand of your enemies. My fervent prayer is that you'll be freed soon by the Eternal One, and lately I have felt a hint of consolation, the gentlest breeze of hope" (Bar 4:21–22).

Psalm Response: "It seemed like a dream, too good to be true, / when GOD returned Zion's exiles. / We laughed, we sang, / we couldn't believe our good fortune. / We were the talk of the nations— / 'GOD was wonderful to them!' / GOD *was* wonderful to us; / we are one happy people." (Ps 126:1–3)

Meditation/Journal: What is meant by "hint of consolation"? Have you ever felt a hint of consolation from God? Explain. What is meant by "gentlest breeze of hope"? Have you ever felt the gentlest breeze of hope in God? Explain.

Prayer: Based on biblical history, I know that you, O Lord, rescued your people from exile and brought them back to Jerusalem (Zion). When I experience troubles of any kind, give me a hint of your consolation. Blow upon me your Holy Spirit, that the gentlest breeze of hope may fill my mind and heart. Hear my prayer today, tomorrow, and forever. Amen.

Mercy and Righteousness

Scripture: "Arise, O Jerusalem, stand upon the height; / look toward the east, / and see your children gathered from west and east / at the word of the Holy One, / rejoicing that God has remembered them. / For they went out from you on foot, / led away by their enemies; / but God will bring them back to you, / carried in glory, as on a royal throne. / For God will lead

Israel with joy, / in the light of his glory, / with the mercy and righteousness that come from him." (Bar 5:5-6, 9)

Reflection: The book of the prophet Baruch is considered part of the OT (A) by Protestants, but it is considered part of the HB (OT) by Catholics, and, as such, is placed in Bibles after Jeremiah and Lamentations, because Baruch is mentioned as Jeremiah's secretary in the book of the prophet Jeremiah (32:12–13, 16; 36:4–5, 8, 10, 13–19, 26–27, 32; 43:3, 6; 45:1–2). The passage above is taken from the fourth of four major parts of the book of Baruch; it is known as the Zion poem (Bar 4:5—5:9). The Zion poem has been influenced by Isaiah 40–66 and Deuteronomy 28–32. The basic idea expressed in the poem is that the Jews of the exile looked back on the sin of their ancestors and, through penitence, could look forward to a return to God. It is called the Zion poem, because Jerusalem is personified as a grieving widow (Bar 4:9–29). In a subsection of the fourth part, Jerusalem is addressed and assured of deliverance (Bar 4:30—5:9). It is from that personification that the above passage comes.

At the time this passage was composed, the Jewish exile was over; some Jews had returned to Jerusalem. Therefore, the unknown author can tell the holy city to climb to the top of a mountain and to look toward the east (Babylon, sunrise) and see her children, the former exiles, gathered from the whole world (west) and Babylon (east) at God's word; they are happy that he has remembered them. Peterson states that they are "rejoicing in the memory of God" (Bar 5:5). He continues: "They were abducted a long time ago by their enemies and led away, made to walk the many miles on foot. God, however, will lead them back to you, carried with glory as though on a royal throne" (Bar 5:6). Israel has repented, and God has repented. Thus, "God will lead Israel home with joy," states Peterson, "lighting the way with the majesty, mercy, and justice only he can command" (Bar 5:9). Majesty refers to God's role as king of Israel. Mercy refers to the compassion, kindness, and forgiveness he has had for his people. And justice refers to the fact that God gave his people what he judged them to deserve by letting them be conquered by their enemies and exiled. Righteousness, meaning to do the right thing because it is the right thing to do—in this case, to bring back the exiles from Babylon to Jerusalem—better expresses the meaning of the word.

Psalm Response: "GOD! God! I am running to you for dear life; / the chase is wild. / If they catch me, I'm finished: / ripped to shreds by foes fierce as lions,

/ dragged into the forest and left / unlooked for, unremembered. / Stand up, GOD; pit your holy fury / against my furious enemies." (Ps 7:1–2, 6)

Meditation/Journal: What has been your most recent experience of God remembering you? What mercy did you receive? What righteousness did you receive?

Prayer: Everlasting God, in joy you brought back to Jerusalem your people who had been taken into Babylonian captivity. When I stray from you, bring me back into your presence. Grant that I may experience your boundless mercy and righteousness today, tomorrow, and forever. Amen.

Mercy not Withdrawn

Scripture: "For your name's sake do not give us up forever [, O Lord,]; / and do not annul your covenant. / Do not withdraw your mercy from us, / for the sake of Abraham your beloved / and for the sake of your servant Isaac / and Israel your holy one, / to whom you promised / to multiply their descendants like the stars of heaven / and like the sand on the shore of the sea. / For we, O Lord, have become fewer / than any other nation, / and are brought low this day in all the world because of our sins." (Sg Three 1:11–14 [Dan 3:34–37])

Reflection: The above passage comes from the OT (A) Prayer of Azariah (Sg Three 1:3–22), which appears in Catholic Bibles in the HB (OT) book of Daniel (3:26–45) but not in Protestant or Jewish bibles. Written in the mid-second century BCE, it is in the form of a national or communal lament, appealing to God for mercy at a time of crisis. The prayer is set during the Babylonian exile and in the context of three young Jews' refusal to worship a golden statue erected by King Nebuchadnezzar (Dan 3:1–23). Shadrach (Hananiah), Meshach (Mishael), and Abednego (Azariah) refuse to worship the statue, and they suffer the penalty of being tossed into a fiery furnace. Azariah's prayer begins by acknowledging God's justice in exiling the Jews to Babylon because they broke the law and tuned away from him (Sg Three 1:4–8 [Dan 3:27–31]). In other words, Azariah acknowledges God's justice; the Jews are exiled because they are getting what they deserve in punishment!

Then, the prayer petitions God not to abandon his people in exile. Peterson states: "Don't ever, we beg you, abandon us—you have promised us otherwise, so please don't water down your covenant" (Dan 3:34). Azariah reminds God of what he promised to Abraham, Isaac, and Israel (Jacob): to multiply their descendants so that they would be as numerous as the stars in the sky or the sand on the seashore. Peterson reminds the reader who Isaac and Israel (Jacob) are in relationship to Abraham and states: "Don't pry your mercy from our grasp; Abraham, your beloved friend, wouldn't want that, nor would his son Isaac or his grandson Israel. You promised that their seed would multiply like the stars in the sky, like the grains of sand on the beach" (Dan 3:35–36). In contrast to the promise of many descendants, Azariah reminds God that the Jews are fewer than any other nation and have been brought low because of their sins. Peterson helps to understand the meaning of Sg Three 1:14, writing, "So why, O Lord, are we now the least favored nation? Why are we ranked lowest of the low? It has to be because of our sins" (Dan 3:37). Azariah concludes his prayer by expressing contrition on behalf of the Jewish nation and its renewed resolve to follow its God, if he does not withdraw his mercy (Sg Three 1:16–22 [Dan 3:39–45]).

Psalm Response: "We've been hearing about this, God, / all our lives. / Our fathers told us the stories / their fathers told them . . . . / All day we parade God's praise— / we thank you by name over and over. / But now you've walked off and left us, / you've disgraced us and won't fight for us. / Get up, GOD! Are you going to sleep all day? / Wake up! Don't you care what happens to us? / Get up and come to our rescue. / If you love us so much, *Help us!* (Ps 44:1, 8–9, 23, 26)

Meditation/Journal: When have you felt like God's mercy had been withdrawn from you? Explain What made you realize that mercy had not been withdrawn from you?

Prayer: O Lord, God of my ancestors, glorious forever is your name. Bestow your mercy upon me, and fill me with your praise today, tomorrow, and forever. Amen.

Find Mercy

Scripture: O Lord, "In our day we have no ruler, or prophet, or leader, / no burnt offering, or sacrifice, or oblation, or incense, / no place to make an offering before you and to find mercy. Yet with a contrite heart and a humble spirit may we be accepted...." (Sg Three 1:15-16 [Dan 3:38-39a])

Reflection: The above passage comes from the OT (A) Prayer of Azariah (Sg Three 1:3-22), which appears in Catholic Bibles in the HB (OT) book of Daniel (3:26-45) but not in Protestant or Jewish bibles. Written in the mid-second century BCE, it is in the form of a national or communal lament, appealing to God for mercy at a time of crisis. The prayer is set during the Babylonian exile and in the context of three young Jews' refusal to worship a golden statue erected by King Nebuchadnezzar (Dan 3:1-23). Shadrach (Hananiah), Meshach (Mishael), and Abednego (Azariah) refuse to worship the statue, and they suffer the penalty of being tossed into a fiery furnace. Azariah begins to pray. In the section of the prayer above, Azariah continues with a description of life in exile. The Jews have no Jewish ruler. The last two kings of Judah—Jehoiachin and Zedekiah—had been taken to Babylon by King Nebuchadnezzar; there they died without descendants. The Jews have no prophet. They failed to listen to their last prophet—Jeremiah—and that is why they found themselves exiled. However, they do have Ezekiel, who accompanied the Jews to Babylon. Because prophecy was understood to have ceased during the exilic period, the author's note indicates that this prayer was a later insertion into the book of Daniel. They have no leader; they have no one to follow; all the potential leaders, like everyone else, were captives of war.

Just like they have no ruler, prophet, or leader, they also have no burnt offering, sacrifice, oblation, incense, or place to make an offering. In other words, sacrifice of any kind was legitimate only in the Jerusalem Temple; in exile there was no place to worship, to find divine mercy. Because there is no legitimate place to make an offering, all the Jews can do is appear before God with a contrite heart and a humble spirit. Thus, Azariah's prayer offers not only the three young men's contrition, but it also offers God their lives in the furnace. Their imminent martyrdom becomes the substitute sacrifice for sin. With such an offering, they hope to find mercy. Peterson states, O Lord, "look upon our contrite heart and humble spirit.... Let our bodies be our sacrifice in your sight today, so that we can follow you perfectly—perfectly in the sense that those who put their faith in you are never wrong" (Dan 3:39-40). Azariah's prayer is heard; all three men emerge from the furnace unburned (Sg Three 1:27 [Dan 3: 50]). They found mercy.

Psalm Response: "Hananiah, Azariah, Mishael—we bless the Lord; we praise and honor him forever. For he rescued us from the world below and saved us from the hand of death; he freed us from the fiery furnace. Stand up and proclaim the greatness of the Lord; he is goodness itself and his mercy never quits. All who are in awe of the God of gods, bless the Lord; stand up and proclaim him, for his mercy never quits." (Sg Three 1:66–68 [Dan 3:88–90])

Meditation/Journal: When have you found yourself all alone and praying for divine mercy? Explain. How did it appear for you? From what were you rescued by God?

Prayer: Lord God, you alone are glorious over the whole world. I sing praise to you and highly exalt you forever. You are good, and your mercy endures forever. I give you thanks for enabling me to find your mercy, which endures forever and ever. Amen.

Asking for Mercy 1

Scripture: ". . . Judas [called Maccabeus] and his brothers saw that misfortunes had increased and that the forces [of King Antiochus Epiphanes under the command of Lysias, who was in charge of the king's affairs,] were encamped in their territory. They also learned what the king had commanded to do to the people to cause their final destruction. But they said to one another, 'Let us restore the ruins of our people and fight for our people and the sanctuary.' So the congregation assembled to be ready for battle, and to pray and ask for mercy and compassion." (1 Macc 3:42–44)

Reflection: After Alexander the Great died, his empire was divided between his army generals. Syria came under the control of Antiochus IV Epiphanes in 175 BCE. Antiochus desired to suppress Jewish worship and way of life and replace it with the Greek pantheon and way of life. In so doing, he encountered the resistance of the Jews. In time, the resistance was led by Judas Maccabeus, who, as the above passage indicates, rallied the Jews to form an army to fight the forces King Antiochus had placed under the command of Lysias to destroy the Jewish residents of Judea and Jerusalem. Lysias was told "to wipe out and destroy the strength of Israel and the remnant of Jerusalem; he was to banish the memory of them from the place, settle aliens in all their territory, and distribute their land by lot"

(1 Macc 3:35–36). When Judas heard what Antiochus wanted Lysias to do, he called the people to restore the ruins and fight for the Jewish people and the Temple, which had been pillaged by Antiochus (1 Macc 1:21–23) and defiled (1 Macc 1:45–61). Antiochus' actions precipitated the Jewish revolt (1 Macc 1:62–64). To squelch the revolt, Antiochus sent forty thousand infantry and seven thousand calvary into Judah. Judas organized the Jews and got them ready to resist; they prayed to God and asked for mercy and compassion (NAB). And with only three thousand men (1 Macc 4:6), Judas defeated Lysias' forces.

The First Book of Maccabees, a type of historical chronicle, is told to glorify the Maccabean leaders, who function as a type of ruling family. While the book was written sometime during the second century BCE, its focus is on politics, power, and the establishment of a Jewish state. The book was never accepted into the Hebrew Bible, but it did find a home in the Christian Hebrew Bible or the Christian Old Testament. In the passage above, it becomes clear that mercy is manifested in military victory, which brings liberation to the Jews. The author assumes that enemies of the Jews are enemies of God, who is the champion of the Jewish nation, which is coming to a new birth under the Maccabean leadership. The Maccabean triumph reflects the favor of God.

Psalm Response: "Oh God, what shall be do . . . ? For your Sanctuary has been trampled and contaminated, your priests are paralyzed with grief and shame. Look, Gentile nations converge against us; they want to destroy us. But you already know what they want to do with us. How shall we resist their attack if you don't help us?" (1 Macc 3:50–53)

Meditation/Journal: What do think about mercy being manifested in military victory? Explain. What modern equivalents of the concept can you think? Do you think triumph reflects God's favor? Explain.

Prayer: Lord God, throughout biblical literature, you are presented as One who takes care of your chosen people. I pray that you show mercy to all peoples and give all peoples the opportunity to respond to you in their own way today, tomorrow, and forever. Amen.

APOCRYPHA/DEUTEROCANONICALS

Mercy Endures Forever

Scripture: "... Gorgias [, a Friend of the king, chosen by Lysias, who oversaw King Antiochus' affairs, to command a division of the king's army] took five thousand infantry and one thousand picked cavalry, and this division moved out by night to fall upon the camp of the Jews and attack them suddenly. But Judas heard of it, and he and his warriors moved out to attack the king's force.... When Gorgias entered the camp of Judas by night, he found no one there, so he looked for them in the hills.... At daybreak Judas appeared in the plain with three thousand men.... Judas said to those who were with him, '... [L]et us cry to Heaven, to see whether he will favor us and remember his covenant with our ancestors and crush this army before us today.'... The Gentiles were crushed, and fled into the plain. [Judas and his men] pursued them ... and three thousand of them fell. Then Judas and his force turned back from pursuing them, and he said to the people, ... 'Gorgias and his force are near us in the hills. But stand now against our enemies and fight them, afterward seize the plunder boldly.' Just as Judas was finishing this speech, a detachment appeared, coming out of the hills. They saw ... the Jews were burning the camp ... and when they also saw the army of Judas drawn up in the plain for battle, they all fled.... Then Judas returned to plunder the camp, and they seized a great amount of gold and silver, and cloth dyed blue and sea purple, and great riches. On their return they sang hymns and praises to Heaven—'For he is good, for his mercy endures forever.' Thus Israel had a great deliverance that day." (1 Macc 4:1–2a, 3, 5–6, 8, 10, 14–16, 18–19, 21–25)

Reflection: In the lengthy, edited biblical passage above from the First Book of Maccabees, written between 134 and 104 BCE, to glorify the dynasty established by the Maccabees—a book not found in the Protestant HB (OT), because it is not found in the Jewish Bible, but found in the Catholic Bible—Judas Maccabeus is presented as an army commander who outmaneuvered his Gentile opponents. Before he prays for divine help, the narrator tells the reader that he has three thousand men—three is the number for God—going against Gorgias' six thousand men—six is an incomplete number—and, thus, the reader concludes that God is on Judas' side! Then, Judas prays that God (Heaven) will favor him and his army and enable them to crush their enemy. He reminds them of how God saved their ancestors at the Sea of Reeds and crushed Pharaoh and his army (1 Macc 4:9). Peterson captures Judas' words this way: "Now's the time to shout to high Heaven!

[The Lord] will have mercy on us. He'll remember our covenant with God. He'll destroy the enemy right under our very nose" (1 Macc 4:10). And that is exactly what happened!

Because Gorgias left his camp unguarded, Judas' army set it on fire. When Gorgias and his army emerge out of the hills, where they went in search of Judas and his army, they see not only the camp burning, but Judas' forces ready for battle, and they flee. Meanwhile, once the fires are out, Judas and his army plunder Gorgias' camp. Then, they praise God's mercy, which has caused their enemy to run away. The victory is not attributed to Judas' superior tactics, but to the power of God's mercy. Peterson captures the excitement of the scene: "Judas and his men visited the abandoned Gentile camp and picked up a fair amount of the spoils of war: gold, silver, some blue and crimson silk, piles of unusual but expensive trinkets. Returning to their base camp, the Jews sang songs and blessed Heaven. 'God is good; his mercy is forever!' From that day forward there was a great sense of security in Israel for quite a while" (1 Macc 4:23–25). NAB states that they were glorifying Heaven (God). The victory song sung by Judas and his army comes from Psalm 118, the Psalm Response below.

Psalm Response: "Thank GOD because he's good, / because his love never quits. / Tell the world, Israel, 'His love never quits.' / And you who fear GOD, join in, 'His love never quits.' / Pushed to the wall, I called to GOD; / from the wide open spaces, he answered. / Far better to take refuge in GOD / than trust in people. / Hemmed in by barbarians, / in GOD's name I rubbed their faces in the dirt . . . . / GOD's my strength, he's also my song, / and now he's my salvation. / Hear the shouts, hear the triumph songs / in the camp of the saved? / 'The hand of GOD has turned the tide! / The hand of GOD is raised in victory! / The hand of God has turned the tide!'" (Ps 118, 1–2, 4–5, 8, 10, 14, 15–16)

Meditation/Journal: In what specific experience of your life have you discovered that God's mercy endures forever? Explain. Specifically, how did God's hand turn the tide in your experience?

Prayer: I give thanks to you, O God, because your steadfast love and mercy endure forever. When I put my trust in you, I am never disappointed; you always come to my aid. Today, tomorrow, and forever I give thanks to you, my God, for you are good and your love and mercy are everlasting. Amen.

Apocrypha/Deuterocanonicals

Mercy for Mercy

Scripture: "In those days Simon encamped against Gazara and surrounded it with troops. He made a siege engine, brought it to the city, and battered and captured one tower. The men in the siege engine leaped out into the city, and a great tumult arose in the city. The men in the city, with their wives and children, went up on the wall with their clothes torn, and they cried out with a loud voice, asking Simon to make peace with them; they said, 'Do not treat us according to our wicked acts but according to your mercy.'" (1 Macc 13:43–46)

Reflection: As one Maccabee followed another as leader of the Jewish army, more and more battles were won, until 142 BCE, when the author of the First Book of Maccabees determined that, in general, the Gentiles had been defeated. The narrator focuses on Simon, a high priest and a commander and leader of the Jews. Simon is characterized by the narrator as having religious interest. After conquering Gazara (not Gaza), he reached an agreement with the Gentiles living there. After he stopped fighting with the citizens, he expelled them from the city, cleansed it of idols, and "settled in it those who observed the law" (1 Macc 13:48). Observance of the Jewish law was a gesture of Jewish independence from Syrian overlords.

Simon's religious interest is displayed in the way he treats his enemies—the Gentile men, their wives, and children. He does not slaughter them. Those citizens, according to Peterson, shout "at the top of their lungs, begging mercy, asking Simon to give them clemency: 'Don't destroy us the way we tried to destroy you; be merciful to us the way we should have been merciful to you'" (1 Macc 13:45–46). NAB portrays them asking Simon not to treat them according to their evil deeds but according to his mercy. In other words, the mercy showed to Israel by God is requested of Simon by the Gentiles, and Simon agrees to pass on mercy to the citizens of Gazara. Simon did not seek revenge on the Gazara citizens for defending themselves; at their request, he offered them clemency, leniency, an act of mercy in response to the mercy he had received from Heaven.

Psalm Response: "A great calm fell upon Judah / for the rest of Simon's term. / He put the nation before himself, / his reign pleased the people. / His golden reputation served him well. . . . / He expanded the boundaries of his nation; / he was master of his population. / He herded captives into prison camps; / he ruled over Gazara. . . . / He made peace on earth; / in the house of Israel he made great joy. / He reinstated God's Law and / enforced its remedies." (1 Macc 14:4, 6–7, 11, 14)

Meditation/Journal: When have you showed mercy to another the same way God showed mercy to you? When have you not showed mercy—but sought revenge—to another the way God showed mercy to you? Why do you think mercy for mercy is better than revenge for mercy? Explain.

Prayer: God of mercy, your high priest Simon demonstrates that mercy received from you should be showed to others. Fill me with the spirit of clemency that I might show leniency to others, and, in so doing, proclaim your peace on earth today, tomorrow, and forever. Amen.

Heaven's Mercy

Scripture: "John [, son of Simon the high priest,] went up from Gazara and reported to his father Simon what Cendebeus [, King Antiochus' commander-in-chief of the coastal country,] had done [—encamped against Judea]. And Simon called in his two eldest sons Judas and John, and said to them: 'My brothers and I and my father's house have fought the wars of Israel from our youth until this day, and things have prospered in our hands so that we have delivered Israel many times. But now I have grown old, and you by Heaven's mercy are mature in years. Take my place and my brother's, and go out and fight for our nation, and may the help that comes from Heaven be with you.'" (1 Macc 16:1–3)

Reflection: The phrase *Heaven's mercy* (or in NAB "the mercy of Heaven") in the OT (A) book of First Maccabees is a double entendre, a word or phrase with two or more meanings. First of all, throughout the First Book of Maccabees, *Heaven's mercy* is used in place of God or LORD. In other words, the author refrains from using God's name out of respect for that name. Furthermore, he employs the biblical understanding of a three-storied universe. Above the dome of the sky is the heaven, and that is where God was presumed to live. The peace that Simon and, before him, his brothers achieved with the ruling empire was temporary and fragile. Even though the Jews appealed for help from Heaven, Heaven never removed them from the constraints of their political environment nor from the fluctuating power of their neighbors.

The second meaning of *Heaven's mercy* refers to the protection Simon's sons—Judas and John—have received from God throughout the time they were growing. They have grown into mature, young men, who are commissioned by their father to continue the battles to maintain Israel's independence. In other words, the next generation of Maccabees are ready for war. Peterson puts Simon's words to his sons this way: "It's your turn now; you're old enough. Take my place and my brothers' places. Go out and fight for the nation. May Heaven's help be with you" (1 Macc 16:3). Simon's closing line interprets the first use of *Heaven's mercy* as *Heaven's help*. Indeed, any divine help the Jews, especially the Maccabees, have received in fighting their wars for independence is, simultaneously, an act of God's mercy.

Psalm Response: "GOD, it seems you've been our home forever; / long before the mountains were born, / Long before you brought earth itself to birth, / from 'once upon a time' to 'kingdom come'—you are God. Oh! Teach us to live well! / Teach us to live wisely and well! / Surprise us with love at daybreak; / then we'll skip and dance all the day long. / And let the loveliness of our Lord, our God, rest on us, / confirming the work that we do. / Oh, yes. Affirm the work that we do!" (Ps 90:1–2, 12, 14, 17)

Meditation/Journal: When have you recently experienced Heaven's mercy or Heaven's help? Explain.

Prayer: Heaven's help, your mercy precedes and follows me throughout my life. Display your compassion to me, your servant, and let your grace fall upon me that the work of my hands may prosper today, tomorrow, and forever. Amen.

God Shows Mercy

Scripture: "One finds in the records that the prophet Jeremiah ordered those who were being deported [to Babylon] to take some of the fire.... It was also in the same document that the prophet... ordered that the tent and the ark should follow with him, and that he went out to the mountain where Moses had gone up and had seen the inheritance of God. Jeremiah came and found a cave-dwelling, and he brought there the tent and the ark and the altar of incense; then he sealed up the entrance." (2 Macc 2:1, 4–5)

His Mercy Endures Forever

Reflection: As the unknown author of the OT (A) book of Second Maccabees states, his work is an abridgment of a five-volume work by Jason of Cyrene around 160 BCE (2 Macc 2:23). The book begins with two letters, both of which are addressed to the Jews in Egypt, urging them to celebrate Hanukkah, which is the festival of the rededication of the Temple after the Jews return from Babylonian captivity. The passage above comes from the second letter, which has the same purpose. Because Hanukkah is a celebration of light, the author presents (invents?) a legend about fire. According to the legend, some of the priests took some of the fire of the altar with them from the Temple in Jerusalem into Babylonian captivity. They hid it in the hollow of a dry cistern (2 Macc 1:19). When they went to retrieve it to take it back to the rebuilt Temple in Jerusalem, they found a liquid named *nephthar*, meaning purification, called naphtha by most people (2 Macc 1:30–36). The reader needs to keep in mind that the Babylonians were conquered by the Persians; King Cyrus of Persia permitted the Jewish exiles to return to Jerusalem and rebuild their Temple. Fire was the most important element in Persian religion; it represented purification par excellence! The focus, of course, is on God, who from the fire of the first Temple kindles fire in the second Temple and, thus, gives reason for the Jews in Egypt to celebrate the purification of the Temple: Hanukkah. Peterson refers to the liquid in the cistern as "inky black water" (2 Macc 1:20) from which a great fire arose. The miraculous preservation of the fire indicates the approval of God, another reason for the Jews in Egypt to mark Hanukkah. God shows mercy to his people (NAB).

Another part of the legend concerns the prophet Jeremiah, who ordered that the tent, ark, and altar of incense from the first Temple should be brought to Mount Nebo and hidden in a cave. Nebo is where Moses died. Those objects from the Holy of Holies were to be hidden until the Lord decreed otherwise. Just as Moses was buried in a place no one knew, the items from the Temple are buried in a place no one knows. They await a regrouping of Israel, a new exodus. Just like they accompanied the Israelites on their exodus through the desert to the promised land, the three objects represent a hope for restoration. One day God would gather his people in Israel, "and shower them with mercy," states Peterson (2 Macc 2:7). ". . . [T]he Lord would disclose everything that had been done and reveal his majesty" (2 Macc 2:8). Because the first Temple was profaned by King Antiochus IV Epiphanes, the elements from the first Temple placed in the second Temple give the latter the same status as the former. The legend appeals to the antiquity of Jewish religion and the fidelity needed to Jewish ancestors. Those who had returned from exile are given a sense of security and identity as Jews. Therefore, those Jews living in Egypt should join those in Jerusalem in celebrating the festival of the purification (rededication) of the (second) Temple. God shows mercy to his people.

Psalm Response: "Lord, Lord God, Creator of everyone and everything, awesome and magnificent, just and merciful, you alone are good. You're the one and only, gracious, just, omnipotent, eternal. You freed Israel from every evil. You picked our forebears to be your chosen people and made them holy. Stand by your people, and they'll stand by you. Gather up the scattered, the Jews in the hinterlands. You'll find many of them are poor and oppressed . . . . Please look kindly on them. Plant your people in your Holy Place, as Moses promised you would do." (2 Macc 1:24–25, 27, 29)

Meditation/Journal: When has God showed mercy to you by gathering you with others? What was the occasion? Was fire involved in any way? Explain.

Prayer: LORD, you revealed yourself to Moses in a bush that burned but was not consumed. Sacrifices made to you were consumed in fire and received invisibly by you, who are invisible. In sacred places around the world marking your presence, gather people and show them your mercy today, tomorrow, and forever. Amen.

Hope for Mercy 3

Scripture: "Since, therefore, we are about to celebrate the purification, we write to you. Will you therefore please keep the days? It is God who has saved all his people, and has returned the inheritance to all, and the kingship and the priesthood and the consecration, as he promised through the law. We have hope in God that he will soon have mercy on us and will gather us from everywhere under heaven into his holy place, for he has rescued us from great evils and has purified the place." (2 Macc 2:16–18)

Reflection: The last 3 verses of the second letter inviting Jews living in Egypt to celebrate Hanukkah in the OT (A) Second Book of Maccabees are found in the passage above. Since the Jews in Jerusalem are getting ready to celebrate Hanukkah (usually in late November or December), they are asking the Jews in Egypt to join them in marking the festival. The God in whom the author hopes is also the God who saves his people. Once in the past he saved them from Egyptian slavery. And now he has saved them from Babylonian exile. They have back the land they once inherited. And as of old, they are a kingly, priestly, sanctified people (Exod 19:6). Peterson states: ". . . [Y]ou'd do well to keep holy those . . . days on which we salute God, who freed his people and returned our heritage and restored our kingdom, priesthood, and ceremonies, just as he promise he would" (2 Macc 2:16–18a).

The hope for mercy is that through a common celebration of Hanukkah by Jews, all will return to the Lord and he will reunite his people. According to NAB, the Lord will show mercy by gathering his people from everywhere. God has acted; he has purified the Temple. The purification can be the first step toward the ingathering of all Jews. It stands for the reversal of the process that began at the time of Jeremiah and the fulfillment of the return. Thus, the letter celebrates the triumph of the Maccabees and the persistence of the Jewish religion, which has overcome the severe crisis of exile and foreign domination. Peterson sates: ". . . [O]ur hope is that after the great evils have passed the Lord will have mercy on us and gather all of us together in Jerusalem where he will have purged the Temple and scoured the holy places" (2 Macc 2:18).

Psalm Response: "Why are you down in the dumps, dear soul? / Why are you crying the blues? / Fix my eyes on God— / soon I'll be praising again. / He puts a smile on my face. / He's my God. / When my soul is in the dumps, I rehearse / everything I know of you . . . . Then GOD promises to love me all day, / sing songs all through the night! / My life is God's prayer." (Ps 42:5–6a, 8)

Meditation/Journal: What hope did you have that was recently fulfilled? What mercy did you receive?

Prayer: I place my hope for mercy in you, O God. Not only do you gather people, but you also fill them with your Spirit. Strengthen me with your Spirit and purify my life that it may be a prayer of praise to you today, tomorrow, and forever. Amen.

Apocrypha/Deuterocanonicals

Mercy as Discipline

Scripture: "... I urge those who read this book not to be depressed by such calamities, but to recognize that ... punishments were designed not to destroy but to discipline our people. In fact, it is a sign of great kindness not to let the impious alone for long, but to punish them immediately. Therefore [the Lord] never withdraws his mercy from us. Although he disciplines us with calamities, he does not forsake his own people." (2 Macc 6:12–13, 16)

Reflection: The author (often called the abbreviator) of the OT (A) book of Second Maccabees tells the reader that he has prepared an abridgment of a five-volume work by Jason of Cyrene (2 Macc 2:23). As certain points in his summary, the author presents his own opinion by intruding his words into the text (4:16–17; 5:17–20). In the passage above, he presents his theology of persecution. He has just finished narrating some of the persecution suffered by the Jews and will present more in what follows the above passage. The misfortunes of the Jews under foreign domination are not by chance but by design, according to the abbreviator. The persecution is divine discipline; God is training, disciplining, educating (and, according to NAB, correcting) his people in how to behave. In other words, God mercifully chastens the Jews before their sins get so great as to warrant destruction. Peterson explains that God has his own ways of being merciful to his own people. No matter what the catastrophe, he never leaves them without help (2 Macc 6:16). The Lord disciplines the Jews; he does not destroy them, states Peterson (2 Macc 16:12). NAB declares that the Lord never withdraws his mercy and does not abandon his own people.

While the author's theological perspective concerning persecution as divine discipline may not sit well with modern people, it is biblical. The motif is found in the HB (OT) book of Deuteronomy (8:5); in the HB (OT) book of Psalms (118:18), in the HB (OT) book of the prophet Isaiah (54:7) and, more explicitly, in the OT (A) book of Wisdom: "... [W]hile chastening us you [, God,] scourge our enemies ten thousand times more, / that, when we judge, we may meditate upon your goodness / and when we are judged, we may expect mercy" (Wis 12:22). According to the abbreviator, God punishes his people now so that they do not become more wayward through lack of discipline, and, consequently, suffer the effect of greater divine wrath later. Because persecutions discipline, they, paradoxically, reflect God's mercy. This theology was designed to help people cope with difficult situations.

Psalm Response: "GOD tested me, he pushed me hard, / but he didn't hand me over to Death. / Thank you for responding to me; / you've truly become my salvation! / The stone the masons discarded as flawed / is now the capstone! / This is GOD's work. / We rub our eyes—we can hardly believe it! / This is the very day GOD acted— / let's celebrate and be festive! / Salvation now, GOD. Salvation now! / O yes, GOD—a free and full life!" (Ps 118:18, 21–25)

Meditation/Response: Do you think God disciplines (shows mercy) through persecution, suffering, and catastrophes? Explain. Have you experienced the merciful discipline of God? How? Explain.

Prayer: By meditating on your goodness to me, O Lord, I recognize the mercy you have bestowed upon me, and in judging others, I desire to show that mercy. When my time to be judged comes, I hope for the same mercy from you. Hear my prayer today, tomorrow, and forever. Amen.

Merciful Life

Scripture: "The mother was especially admirable and worthy of honorable memory. Although she saw her seven sons perish within a single day, she bore it with good courage because of her hope in the Lord. Filled with a noble spirit, she reinforced her woman's reasoning with a man's courage, and said to them, '... [T]he Creator of the world, who shaped the beginning of humankind and devised the origin of all things, will in his mercy give life and breath back to you again, since you now forget yourselves for the sake of his laws.'" (2 Macc 7:20, 21b, 23)

Reflection: The centerpiece of the OT (A) Second Book of Maccabees is the account of a Jewish mother and her seven sons, who are arrested and brought before King Antiochus because they refuse to eat pork (2 Macc 7:1). As the legend is narrated, the author presents a theology of martyrdom. There are seven sons because seven represents perfection; here is a perfect Jewish family dying rather than violate Jewish law. The first principle of martyrdom is the readiness to die rather than transgress ancestral Jewish laws—in this case, eating pork. The second principle is the hope of resurrection. The third principle is that martyrs suffer for the sins of the Jewish people collectively. And the fourth principle is introduced by the mother in the above passage. Her seven sons owe their lives to their

Creator, from whom they hope to get them back. In other words, death must be accepted if the afterlife is to follow. In his great mercy, the Lord gives life and breath back to those who die, just like he gave life and breath to each of the woman's sons in her womb. Peterson captures the emotion of the scene by portraying the mother stating: "I don't know how you all appeared in my womb; I wasn't the one who gave you life and breath, and I didn't give you shape or form. The Creator of the world did that. He's the one who made the first human and everything else in the universe; he's the one who'll restore all of you, body and soul, because you loved him more than your lives" (2 Macc 7:22–23). According to the mother in NAB, God will do this in his mercy.

The mother of seven sons is, according to the author, to be admired; she is worthy of honorable memory. She, a woman—considered a weaker vessel in Jewish culture—is made of stern stuff! King Antiochus, a man, is bested by a woman, who dies after the last of her seven sons (2 Macc 7:24–40). The story leads the reader to consider his or her emotions concerning suffering, death, and admiration. Such a story inspired the Jews during times of persecution. They are exhorted to remain faithful to their laws, just like the seven sons and their mother did in the story. In his mercy, the Lord will give life and breath back to those who die for their faith.

Psalm Response: "Quick, GOD, I need your helping hand! / The last decent person just went down, / All the friends I depend on gone. / Everyone talks in lie language; / Lies slide off their oily lips. / They doubletalk with forked tongues. / Into the hovels of the poor, / Into the dark streets where the homeless groan, God speaks: / 'I've had enough; I'm on my way / To heal the ache in the heart of the wretched.'" (Ps 12:1–2, 5)

Meditation/Journal: Identify one person you admire who faces obstacles with courage and hope. How does he/she do it? Identify one person you admire for his/her faith. How does he/she express that faith?

Prayer: Lord, I turn my gaze from the earth to the heavens to admire everything you have made from nothing, including me! Give me the courage of the mother, who watched her seven sons be put to death before her, and give me the faith all of them possessed in the resurrection. I hope to see you one day at the time of divine mercy to come, when you will restore breath and life to everything you have created. Amen.

Time of Mercy

Scripture: "The youngest brother being still alive, Antiochus not only appealed to him in words, but promised with oaths that he would make him rich and enviable if he would turn from the ways of his ancestors, and that he would take him for his Friend and entrust him with public affairs. Since the young man would not listen to him at all, the king called the mother to him and urged her to advise the youth to save himself. . . . [S]he spoke in their native language as follows, deriding the cruel tyrant: 'My son, have pity on me. I carried you nine months in my womb, and nursed you for three years, and have reared you and brought you up to this point in your life, and have taken care of you. Do not fear this butcher, but prove worthy of your [six] brothers. Accept death, so that in God's mercy I may get you back again along with your brothers.'" (2 Macc 7:24b–27, 29)

Reflection: As the story of the seven brothers and their mother continues to unfold in the OT (A) book of Second Maccabees, King Antiochus, after overseeing the death of six brothers, attempts to convince the youngest brother to save himself. First, he promises riches and other things. Second, he urges the young man's mother to convince him to save himself. She, however, deceives the king by speaking to her son in Hebrew—a language Antiochus doesn't understand—to remain steadfast in his Jewish faith. She recounts all she had done for him, then she urges him to acknowledge all that God has done for him. Finally, she tells him to follow in the path of his brothers and accept death. Then, God will show his mercy to him, his brothers, and his mother by raising them from the dead. NAB refers to God's action as the time of mercy. She tells her son not to fear Antiochus, who had presented him with false hopes; no matter living or dead he cannot escape from God!

The mother's words to her youngest son emphasize that there is no reason to fear a human tyrant, like Antiochus. God, whom she identifies as the creator of the human race, is the One upon whom everyone is dependent. In other words, attributing creation to God puts human life in perspective. That is why the mother tells her son the exact opposite of what the king had suggested. Peterson phrases her words in this way: "No need to fear him; he's just a butcher. I want you to be worthy of your brothers and join them in their death. As for me, I look forward to seeing you all in the time of divine mercy to come" (2 Macc 7:29). Because the youngest son owes his life to the Creator, he can hope to get it back from God again, when God displays mercy in the future, according to the young man's mother.

Psalm Response: "O Lord Almighty, / God of our ancestors, of Abraham and Isaac and Jacob / and of their righteous offspring; / you who made heaven and earth / with all their order; / yet immeasurable and unsearchable is your promised mercy, for you are the Lord Most High, / of great compassion, long-suffering, and very merciful, / and you relent at human suffering. / O Lord, according to your great goodness / you have promised repentance and forgiveness / to those who have sinned against you, / and in the multitude of your mercies, / you have appointed repentance for sinners, / so that they may be saved." (NRSV, Pr Man 1:1–2, 6–8)

Meditation/Journal: Can you save yourself? Explain. Who has presented you with false hopes? Explain. According to the Prayer of Manasseh, the Psalm Response above, how does God save? Do you agree or disagree? Explain.

Prayer: O Lord, I look at the underworld, the earth, and the heavens you created, along with everything that is in them, and I recognize that you made them out of nothing. In the same way I came into being, and I know that one day my body will go out of existence. I trust that in your great mercy you will raise me to life again. Amen.

Show Mercy Soon

Scripture: "While [his mother] was still speaking, the young man said, . . . 'I, like my brothers, give up body and life for the laws of our ancestors, appealing to God to show mercy soon to our nation and by trials and plagues to make you [, Antiochus,] confess that he alone is God, and through me and my brothers to bring to an end the wrath of the Almighty that has justly fallen on our whole nation.'" (2 Macc 7:30a, 37–38)

Reflection: The most powerful speech of all in the story about the seven brothers and their mother in the OT (A) book of Second Maccabees is that of the youngest son. He tells the king that he, like his six brothers before him, willingly gives up his body and spirit in order not to violate the laws of his ancestors about diet (in this case, eating pork). He reaffirms the idea that suffering is divine chastisement (2 Macc 7:32). He appeals to God to show mercy soon to the nation of Israel by bringing to an end the Lord's wrath that has fallen upon it. Peterson presents the youngest son's words this way: "We've endured the suffering because we committed the sins. Yes, God's angry with our people, but it's for our own good and only for a little while; then we'll be reconciled with him again" (2 Macc 7:32–33). In other words, the punishment of the nation was just, and the sufferings of the martyrs (the seven sons and their mother) absorb the punishment and bring them to an end.

The youngest son states that he hopes that God will send trials and plagues to make King Antiochus confess that the Lord alone is God. Should this be done, the persecution would end, and God's wrath would cease. "I invoke God," states the youngest brother, according to Peterson, "to hasten his mercy; the stripes and welts are my confession that he's the Lord, the one and only. My family deserves the punishment of the Almighty for our sins and the sins of our people, but it shall soon be over for us. But not for you" (2 Macc 7:38). In other words, after Antiochus is tormented—like he has been tormenting the Jews—he will want to be a Jew and acknowledge the God of the Jews (2 Macc 9:17). As the narrative of the Second Book of Maccabees continues, God's wrath stops (2 Macc 8:5), and the Jews under the leadership of Judas Maccabeus will begin to be unstoppable. The story of the seven brothers and their mother ends with words of the narrator: "So [the youngest brother] died in his integrity, putting his whole trust in the Lord. Last of all, the mother died, after her sons" (2 Macc 7:40–41). NAB states that the youngest son died undefiled, putting all his trust in God.

Psalm Response: "[O Lord,] . . . I bend the knee of my heart, / imploring you for your kindness. / For you, O Lord, are the God of those who repent, / and in me you will manifest your goodness; / for, unworthy as I am, you will save me / according to your great mercy, / and I will praise you continually all the days of my life." (NRSV, Pr Man 1:11, 13d–15a)

Meditation/Journal: When have you considered suffering for your own good? Explain. How did your suffering proclaim God? How did it lead you to put your trust in God?

Prayer: After enduring brief suffering, you bestow ever-flowing life upon your people, O God. When I am suffering, show me your mercy. Hear my petition and listen for my words of praise today, tomorrow, and forever. Amen.

Apocrypha/Deuterocanonicals

Pity and Mercy

Scripture: "[Meanwhile Judas and his companions] implored the Lord to look upon the people who were oppressed by all; and to have pity on the temple that had been profaned by the godless; to have mercy on the city that was being destroyed and about to be leveled to the ground; to hearken to the blood that cried out to him, and to remember also the lawless destruction of the innocent babies and the blasphemies committed against his name; and to show his hatred of evil." (2 Macc 8:2–4)

Reflection: After finishing the story about the seven sons and their mother, the abbreviator of the OT (A) Second Book of Maccabees resumes the story about Judas Maccabeus, whom he had mentioned in 5:27. Peterson refers to Judas as the Hammer, the meaning of the Hebrew word and the description of what Judas and his men will do, with God's help, to the Gentiles occupying their land. Only Peterson presents verse 2 through 4 as a prayer in the first person. NRSV above and NAB present the prayer in third-person narrative. In either case, the prayer echoes the words of the seventh brother (2 Macc 7:37). First, in the prayer, God is called upon to see (a) his oppressed people. Earlier, the author had stated that God "never withdraws his mercy" from his people (2 Macc 6:16). God is implored (b) to see and have pity on the temple that had been profaned by the installation of a statue of Zeus by King Antiochus; NAB refers to the sanctuary as the place where God dwelt in the Holy of Holies of the Temple. God is called upon to see and have mercy (3) on Jerusalem, the city that was being, in Peterson's words, ruined and leveled. Second, in the prayer, God is asked to listen to the bleeding voices rising to him (Peterson), like Abel's blood that cried out from the ground (Gen 4:10). Third, in the prayer God is asked to remember (a) the destruction of children, the criminal slaughter of innocent children (according to NAB), when King Antiochus took Jerusalem (2 Macc 5:13). He is also asked to remember (b) the blasphemies committed against his name; however, at this point in the story, no blasphemies have been uttered. And, fourth, to manifest his hatred of evil (NAB)—evil being the Greek overlords—God is asked to defeat the occupiers of the land.

Thus, before the military campaign begins, Judas and his followers give voice to a prayer that indicates what finally turns the tide. Oppression and profanation have gone far enough. Jerusalem has been adequately punished by Greek persecutors. God will endure no more insult; it's time for God to act on behalf of babies and martyrs. Judas Maccabeus is the instrument of

God's deliverance. At this point in the story, Judas, his brothers, and his guerrilla band become the focus for how God saves his people—how God shows pity and mercy.

Psalm Response: "I love you, GOD— / you make me strong. / GOD is bedrock under my feet, / the castle in which I live, / my rescuing knight. / My God—the high crag / where I run for dear life, / hiding behind the boulders, / safe in the granite hideout. / I sing to GOD, the Praise-Lofty, / and find myself safe and saved." (Ps 18:1–3)

Meditation/Journal: Based on a recent experience, write a prayer that petitions God to see, listen, remember, and manifest his hatred for evil. Or, what experience in your life brought you to implore God to see what was going on, to listen to your prayer, to remember something that happened, and to manifest his love for good?

Prayer: Lord, see me reflecting upon your word in the Second Book of Maccabees. Listen to my prayer for pity and mercy, as I remember all your gifts to me. Grant me the grace to engage in good works that glorify your name today, tomorrow, and forever. Amen.

Wrath Turned to Mercy

Scripture: "As soon as [Judas] Maccabeus got his army organized, the Gentiles could not withstand him for the wrath of the Lord had turned to mercy." (2 Macc 8:5)

Reflection: With the verse above, the OT (A) Second Book of Maccabees changes focus. The persecution of the Jews by the Gentiles—called God's wrath—becomes the legitimate persecution of Gentiles by the Jews—called God's mercy! In other words, the story of the Jewish revolt begins. Its leader, Judas, employs hit-and-run methods (2 Macc 8:6–7), but, echoing the seventh son's words (2 Macc 7:38), God's wrath becomes God's mercy. Peterson records the narrative this way: ". . . God redirected his anger from the Jews to the Gentiles; the foreign occupiers became no match for the Jewish forces" (2 Macc 8:5).

The daring bravery of Judas infects and inspires his army (2 Macc 8:16). In one speech, Judas states that the Gentiles trust in their arms and acts of daring, but the Jews "trust in the Almighty God, who is able with a single nod to strike down those" who were coming against them (2 Macc 8:18). Peterson captures Judas' focus off himself and onto God, narrating, "Judas rallied his troops . . . and told them not to worry; yes, they were outnumbered, but God was on their side, fighting side by side with the men around him, just like one of them" (2 Macc 8:16). Judas' focus on God is also found in the watchword: "The help of God" (2 Macc 8:23). Peterson records Judas' words to his troops this way: "The only thing our enemies trust is their weapons and their battle screams. We, however, pray to and solely rely on the Almighty God, who at his discretion can destroy an entire army . . . with a nod of his head" (2 Macc 8:18). The narrator of the book states: "With these words [Judas] filled [his forces] with courage and made them ready to die for their laws and their country . . ." (2 Macc 8:21), all because the Jews perceived that God's wrath had turned to mercy.

Psalm Response: "Good people, cheer GOD! / Right-living people sound best when praising. / Use guitars to reinforce your Hallelujahs! / Play his praise on a grand piano! / Invent your own new song to him; / give him a trumpet fanfare. / Watch this: God's eye is on those who respect him, / the ones who are looking for his love. / He's ready to come to their rescue in bad times; in lean times he keeps body and soul together." (Ps 33:1–3, 18–19)

Meditation/Journal: When have you experienced God being on your side? Explain.

Prayer: While others trust in their investments, positions, and reputation, I place all my trust in you, Almighty God. With your Holy Spirit strengthen that trust, and out of your mercy give me the courage to bear witness to your name today, tomorrow, and forever. Amen.

Beginning of Mercy

Scripture: "When [Judas Maccabeus and his forces] had collected the arms of the enemy and stripped them of their spoils, they kept the sabbath, giving great praise and thanks to the Lord, who had preserved them for that day and allotted it to them as the beginning of mercy." (2 Macc 8:27)

Reflection: The phrase *the beginning of mercy*, found in the above verse from OT (A) Second Book of Maccabees—and also found in NAB—refers back to 2 Macc 8:5 (above), where the narrator notes that God's anger had turned to mercy; also, it looks forward to 2 Macc 8:29: "When [the Jewish army] had [collected weapons and loot], they made common supplication and implored the merciful Lord to be wholly reconciled with his servants." Peterson states, "It was the beginning of a brand new era of the Lord's mercy on the house of Israel" (2 Macc 8:27). The focus of the verse is not on Maccabeus and his forces winning the battle; rather, the focus is on God, who defends those who keep his laws and makes them invincible. That is why the narrator of the story states that the day was getting late as the forces collected their enemy's weapons and removed valuables from their dead bodies. After they hurried, they observed the sabbath, which demonstrates their piety to God's law. Their devotion to God is further emphasized by the mention of them giving some of the spoils to those who had been tortured, widows, and orphans (2 Macc 8:28).

When it comes to facing the Gentiles, the Jewish army is scarcely necessary! God is the champion of his people, who are invulnerable because they follow God's laws, as in keeping the sabbath. Furthermore, the act of observing the sabbath is designed to persuade readers to cheer for the Jewish underdogs, while laughing at the powerful forces God defeated! A small force can be victorious. According to the narrator, "With the Almighty as their ally, they killed more than nine thousand of the enemy, and wounded and disabled most of . . . [the] army, and forced them all to flee" (2 Macc 8:24).

Psalm Response: "[God] shows me how to fight; / I can bend a bronze bow! / You protect me with salvation-armor; / you hold me up with a firm hand, / caress me with your gentle ways. / You cleared the ground under me / so my footing was firm/ When I chased my enemies I caught them; / I didn't let go till they were dead men. / I nailed them; they were down for good; / then I walked all over them. / You armed me well for this fight, / you smashed the upstarts. / You made my enemies turn tail, / and I wiped out the haters. / They yelled for GOD / and got no for an answer." (Ps 18:34–40a, 41)

Meditation/Journal: In what specific ways have you demonstrated the beginning of mercy after winning a battle of some kind?

Prayer: With your help, O God, I can face any obstacle. So, please hear my prayer as I face every crisis and use it to begin your mercy again. Hear my words of praise and thanksgiving for all you do for me today, tomorrow, and forever. Amen.

APOCRYPHA/DEUTEROCANONICALS

No Mercy 6

Scripture: ". . . [T]he all-seeing Lord, the God of Israel, struck [Antiochus IV Epiphanes] with an incurable and invisible blow. Thus he who only a little while before had thought in his superhuman arrogance that he could command the waves of the sea, and had imagined that he could weigh the high mountains in a balance, was brought down to earth and carried in a litter, making the power of God manifest to all. And so the ungodly man's body swarmed with worms, and while he was still living in anguish and pain, his flesh rotted away. Then it was that, broken in spirit, he began to lose much of his arrogance and to come to his senses under the scourge of God, for he was tortured with pain every moment. And when he could not endure his own stench, he uttered these words. 'It is right to be subject to God; mortals should not think that they are equal to God.' Then the abominable fellow made a vow to the Lord, who would no longer have mercy on him, stating that the holy city which he was hurrying to level to the ground and to make a cemetery, he was now declaring to be free . . . ." (2 Macc 9:5a, 8-9, 11-14)

Reflection: The author of the OT (A) book of Second Maccabees takes great delight in narrating the suffering and death of King Antiochus IV Epiphanes. The verses above represent a small sampling from chapter 9. The author is very clear that it is God who strikes down Antiochus and makes his power manifest in that deed. While such a thought may be offensive to modern people, the author of Second Maccabees considers Antiochus' punishment due for the way he treated the Jews, especially because of his arrogance; the greater the arrogance, the greater the humiliation! The affliction Antiochus had inflicted on the Jews is repaid by the affliction God inflicted on Antiochus. In other words, he is repaid. It is only when he was broken in spirit that his arrogance began to dissipate. But even that is attributed to God. His death-bed repentance is, of course, non-historical. It is portrayed in this book because it fulfills the words of the seventh son in the narrative of the seven brothers and their mother above. The seventh son appeals to God to inflict trials and plagues to make Antiochus confess that the Lord alone is God (2 Macc 7:37). But, as the narrator makes clear, the Lord would not have mercy on him! Peterson captures the scene this way: "His pride had been destroyed at last, and there was a moment of self-reflection left. He finally realized that no human beings should ever act as though they were divine. 'It's okay to be slapped around by God, but it's not okay to slap others around as though you were God.' Then this disgusting excuse for a man... began to pray to the one true Lord" (2 Macc 9:11–13).

It is interesting that Peterson leaves out the note about the Lord never again showing mercy to Antiochus (NAB). Nevertheless, the king non-historically voices a vow about stopping the leveling of Jerusalem. Antiochus' plan was to destroy the holy city and turn it into a common graveyard (NAB). If he had accomplished the plan to make it a cemetery, the Jews would not have been able ever to go there again, because it would be unclean or polluted. Antiochus made other promises (2 Macc 9:15–17) including one to become a Jew himself in fulfillment of the seventh son's words, but his sufferings did not abate "for the judgment of God had justly come upon him" (2 Macc 9:18). The author of this book would not allow God to hear the king's prayer! No mercy would be showed to him.

Psalm Response: "How well God must like you— / ... [Y]ou thrill to GOD's Word, / you chew on Scripture day and night. / You're not at all like the wicked, / who are mere windblown dust— / Without defense in court, / unfit company for innocent people. / GOD charts the road you take. / The road *they* take is Skid Row." (Ps 1:1a, 2, 4–6)

Meditation/Journal: What are your thoughts about the author of the Second Book of Maccabees words about God showing no mercy to King Antiochus IV Epiphanes? Do you think God manifests his power by striking down wicked people? Explain. In your self-reflection, what do you like about the Second Book of Maccabees' account of the end of Antiochus?

Prayer: Lord God, in multiple ways you manifest your power in your world, rewarding righteousness and punishing evil. When my spirit is broken, fill me with the spirit of self-reflection that I may correct my ways and conform my will to yours. Hear this prayer today, tomorrow, and forever. Amen.

Angel of Mercy

Scripture: "When Maccabeus and his men got word that Lysias [, King Antiochus Eupator's guardian and kinsman, who was in charge of the government,] was besieging the strongholds, they and all the people, with lamentations and tears, prayed the Lord to send a good angel to save Israel. And... while they were still near Jerusalem, a horseman appeared at their head, clothed in white and brandishing weapons of gold. And together they

Apocrypha/Deuterocanonicals

all praised the merciful God, and were strengthened in heart . . . . They advanced in battle order, having their heavenly ally, for the Lord had mercy on them." (2 Macc 11:6, 8–9, 10)

Reflection: After King Antiochus IV Epiphanes dies, his young son, Antiochus V Eupator, takes his throne under the guardianship of Lysias, who, according to the author of Second Maccabees, "took no account whatever of the power of God, but was elated with his [army and elephants]" (2 Macc 11:4), as he invaded Judea outside of Jerusalem. Judas Maccabeus assembled his forces and prayed that God would send an angel to help them. Peterson notes: "They asked the Lord to send an experienced angel to save them yet again" (2 Macc 11:6). The angel, a representative of God's mercy, led them into battle, with the Lord covering their back (Petrson). They killed many of their enemies, and those they did not kill, including Lysias, fled. Lysias "realized that the Hebrews [Jews] were invincible because the mighty God fought on their side" (2 Macc 11:13). The description of Judas' army advancing in battle order or battle formation emphasizes their trust in the merciful God; in other words, God's mercy—in any form—is necessary for success. In every battle narrated in Second Maccabees, the emphasis is always on God's mercy and help. God, in the form of an angel, fights for the Jews to defeat their enemies.

While many people picture a man or woman with wings, when hearing the word *angel*, that is not what the ancient writer has in mind! In biblical literature, an angel is a code word for God. The angel carries weapons of gold, because gold is the color for divine figures. That detail alone would give ancient readers the information necessary to determine who the angel was. But even more information is given. The angel is dressed in white; that is the color of the Ancient of Days (Ancient One) in the vision of the prophet Daniel (7:9). It is also the color of the robe of the young man sitting in the tomb in Mark's Gospel (16:5), the angel of the Lord in Matthew's Gospel (28:3), and Jesus at his transfiguration (Mark 9:3; Matt 17:2; Luke 9:29). Thus, there is no doubt as to the angel's identity; God has sent himself in response to Judas' prayer. Peterson states that Lysias "didn't have a prayer of beating the Jews as long as they had the all-powerful God back them up" (2 Macc 11:13). The angel's presence furthers the reader's belief that the Jews are invincible, because the author never acknowledges the battles they lost! The sequel to the battle was an agreed-upon peace, in which the Jews were given their religious liberty, because they were led by an angel of mercy.

Psalm Response: "I bless GOD every chance I get; / my lungs expand with his praise. / I live and breathe GOD; / if things aren't going well, hear this and be happy: / GOD's angel sets up a circle / of protection around us while we pray. / Open your mouth and taste, open your eyes and see— / how good GOD is. / Blessed are you who run to him." (Ps 34: 1–2, 7–8)

Meditation/Journal: Have you ever experienced an angel of mercy? Explain.

Prayer: There is no time that I do not need your help, O Lord. Send an angel of mercy to guide me and protect me. Then, you can delight in the welfare you provide, as I praise you for your goodness today, tomorrow, and forever. Amen.

Overtaken by Mercies

Scripture: ". . . [T]he high priest Simon, facing the sanctuary, bending his knees and extending his hands with calm dignity, prayed as follows: . . . 'O holy King, . . . this audacious and profane man undertakes to violate the holy place on earth dedicated to your glorious name. But because you graciously bestowed your glory on your people Israel, you sanctified this place. Wipe away our sins and disperse our errors, and reveal your mercy at this hour. Speedily let your mercies overtake us, and put praises in the mouth of those who are downcast and broken in spirit, and give us peace.'" (3 Macc 2:1, 13–14, 16, 19–20)

Reflection: The Third Book of Maccabees has nothing to do with the Maccabees; rather, it is a story about the Jewish community in Egypt in the third century BCE. Like the Maccabees in Israel, the Jews in Egypt are endangered by hostile gentiles, but they are delivered by God in the end. While Eastern Christianity accepts 3 Maccabees as part of its canon, neither Roman Catholic nor Protestant Christianity accepts it. The above Scripture passage comes from the second of three episodes contained in the OT (A) Third Book of Maccabees. It narrates the attempt of the king of Egypt's—Ptolemy IV Philopater's—attempt to enter the Jerusalem Temple. After his arrival in Jerusalem, he was greeted by the Jews and given gifts. Then, he "conceived a desire to enter the sanctuary" (3 Macc 1:10), which only the high priest—Simon—was allowed to enter. After he was told that he could not enter the sanctuary, he was more determined than ever to do

Apocrypha/Deuterocanonicals

so (3 Macc 1:8–29). That is when Simon, the high priest, began to pray. The passage above is a short selection from his long prayer.

Simon calls upon God to reveal his mercy as quickly as possible. Here, the mercy requested is to stop Philopater from entering the sanctuary and defiling the Temple. Simon asks God to let his mercies overtake the Jews. And that is exactly what God does. Philopater is paralyzed and unable to speak (3 Macc 2:22). He is dragged away by his bodyguards. While the author of Third Maccabees calls it God's "righteous judgment" (3 Macc 2:22), the description given resembles one who is having a stroke. According to the author, "After a while, he recovered, and though he had been punished, he by no means repented, but went away uttering bitter threats" (3 Macc 2:24). After he returned to Egypt, he inflicted public disgrace on the Jewish community, insisted on worship of an idol, imposed a poll tax, and reduced the Jews in the diaspora—those Jews living outside Israel—to the status of slaves. He also ordered that they be branded and more (3 Macc 2:25—5:51).

Psalm Response: "I've already run for dear life / straight to the arms of GOD. / . . . GOD hasn't moved to the mountains; / his holy address hasn't changed. / He's in charge, as always, his eyes / taking everything in, his eyelids / Unblinking, examining Adam's unruly brood / inside and out, not missing a thing. / He tests the good and the bad alike; / if anyone cheats, God's outraged. / Fail the test and you're out, / out in a hail of firestones, / Drinking from a canteen / filled with hot desert wind. / God's business is putting things right; / he loves getting the lines straight, / Setting us straight. Once we're standing tall, / we can look him straight in the eye." (Ps 11:1, 4–7)

Meditation/Journal: When have you been overtaken by God's mercies? Explain. For what did you pray? What did you receive? How fast was your prayer answered?

Prayer: Father of all, you overtake people with your boundless mercies. Your generosity is well known. Hear my prayers and, Holy One among the holy, grant me your merciful grace today, tomorrow, and forever. Amen.

Governing with Mercy

Scripture: Eleazar prayed as follows: "King of great power, Almighty God Most High, governing all creation with mercy, look upon the descendants of Abraham, O Father, upon the children of the sainted Jacob, a people of your consecrated portion who are perishing as foreigners in a foreign land." (3 Macc 6:2–3)

Reflection: The prayer above comes from the third episode in the OT (A) book of Third Maccabees, which is set in Egypt in the third century BCE. The king is Ptolemy IV Philopator, who, after making a trip to Jerusalem and being barred entrance to the Temple, returns to Egypt to persecute the Jews living there (3 Macc 2:25—6:15). After he has all the Jews arrested, he orders them to be enclosed in a hippodrome (3 Macc 4:11). Then, he orders Hermon, keeper of the elephants (3 Macc 5:1), to drug the animals with wine and frankincense and release them in the hippodrome to trample the Jews to death. But at every step taken to enact his plan, he is thwarted by divine intervention. In other words, just like God protected the Hebrews making their escape from Egypt in the HB (OT) Book of Exodus, so God is protecting the Jews in Egypt. Thus, after Hermon gets the elephants ready the first time, he goes to the king to report his preparations. "But the Lord sent upon the king a portion of sleep . . . . And by the action of the Lord he was overcome by so pleasant and deep a sleep that he quite failed in his lawless purpose and was completely frustrated in his inflexible plan" (3 Macc 5:11–12). In other words, God causes the king to sleep through the appointed hour!

Summoning Hermon again, the king tells him to prepare again the elephants (3 Macc 5:20) for the second attempt. The Jews stretch their hands to heaven and implore God to help them. This time God fills the king with incomprehension. According to the author of the story, "This was the act of God who rules over all things, for he had implanted in the king's mind a forgetfulness of the things he had previously devised. . . . [B]y the providence of God his whole mind had been deranged . . ." (3 Macc 5:28, 30). The Jews praise God for the aid they have received, just when King Ptolemy decides to kill them a third time (3 Macc 5:40). The narrator of the story states that after he gets rid of the Jews in Egypt he intends to march on Jerusalem, burn the temple, and render it empty (3 Macc 5:43). The Jews implore God to manifest himself and be merciful to them (3 Macc 5:51). That is when Eleazar takes control of the situation. In the beginning of his prayer, he acknowledges that God governs all creation with mercy. Unlike the king, who governs with death, God governs with life. Ptolemy's plan for death makes the king a mere pawn in God's hand. God governs with mercy that results in life, as we will see below.

APOCRYPHA/DEUTEROCANONICALS

Psalm Response: "GOD, my shepherd! / I don't need a thing. / You have bedded me down in lush meadows, / you find me quiet pools to drink from. / True to your word, / you let me catch my breath / and send me in the right direction. / Even when the way goes through Death Valley, / I'm not afraid when you walk at my side. / Your trusty shepherd's crook makes me feel secure." (Ps 23:1–4)

Meditation/Journal: Where do you see God governing creation with mercy?

Prayer: God Most High, you govern your creation with mercy, showering life everywhere. Pour on me your grace that gives abundant life, and instill in me a deep respect for all the life I see around me. Hear my prayer for your mercy today, tomorrow, and forever. Amen.

Light of Mercy

Scripture: Eleazar prayed: Almighty God Most High, "Pharaoh with his abundance of chariots, the former ruler of this Egypt, exalted with lawless insolence and boastful tongue, you destroyed together with his arrogant army by drowning them in the sea, manifesting the light of your mercy on the nation of Israel." (3 Macc 6:4)

Reflection: The prayer above comes from the third episode in the OT (A) book of Third Maccabees, which is set in Egypt in the third century BCE. The king is Ptolemy IV Philopator, who, after making a trip to Jerusalem and being barred entrance to the Temple, returned to Egypt to persecute the Jews living there (3 Macc 2:25—6:15). After he had all the Jews arrested, he ordered them to be enclosed in a hippodrome (3 Macc 4:11). Then, he ordered Hermon, keeper of the elephants (3 Macc 5:1), to drug the animals with wine and frankincense and release them in the hippodrome to trample the Jews to death. But at every step taken to enact his plan he is thwarted by divine intervention (see above). Just as Ptolemy is about to get his plan enacted—his third attempt—the priest Eleazar appears in the story and immediately takes command of the situation.

As indicated in the passage above, in his prayer Eleazar reminds God that with the light of his mercy he saved the Hebrews who had been enslaved in Egypt. Next, he reminds God that he conquered Sennacherib, king of the Assyrians, when he laid siege to Jerusalem (3 Macc 6:5). Once the Jews were taken into Babylonian captivity, God saved three companions, as narrated in the HB (OT) book of Daniel, from Nebuchadnezzar's fiery furnace (3 Macc 6:6) and the prophet Daniel from the lion's den (3 Macc 6:7). He also mentions the rescue of Jonah from the belly of a sea-born monster (3 Macc 6:8). Eleazar concludes: "And now, you who hate insolence, all-merciful and protector of all, reveal yourself quickly to those of the nation of Israel—who are being outrageously treated by the abominable and lawless Gentiles.... O Eternal One, who have all might and all power, watch over us now and have mercy on us..." (3 Macc 6:9, 12). God hears Eleazar's prayer and reveals himself by sending angels, who confuse the enemy forces, bind them with invisible shackles, and cause the elephants to trample and kill the enemy (3 Macc 6:18–21). Eleazar's prayer reminds God of some of the tyrants in the past whom God humbled and with miraculous deliverance saved his people. Thus, Philopater is humbled (see below) and the Jews are saved by the light of God's mercy—the third time in the Third Book of Maccabees.

Psalm Response: "Let my cry come right into your presence, GOD; / provide me with the insight that comes only from your Word. / Give my request your personal attention, / rescue me on the terms of your promise. / Let praise cascade off my lips; / after all, you've taught me the truth about life! / And let your promises ring from my tongue; / every order you've given is right. / Put your hand out and steady me / since I've chosen to live by your counsel. / I'm homesick, GOD, for your salvation; / I love it when you show yourself!" (Ps 119:169–174)

Meditation/Journal: When has the light of God's mercy shined on you and delivered you from an enemy? Explain. Of what did you remind God in your prayer?

Prayer: Almighty God Most High, you possess all power. Watch over me and shed the light of your mercy upon me. Open my lips in praise of your might today, tomorrow, and forever. Amen.

Mercy Revealed

Scripture: "The king's anger was turned to pity and tears...." He said: "'Loose and untie their unjust bonds! Send them back to their homes in peace, begging pardon for your former actions! Release the children of the almighty and living God of heaven....'... [T]he Jews, immediately released, praised their holy God and Savior, since they now had escaped death. [T]he Lord of all most gloriously revealed his mercy and rescued them all together and unharmed." (3 Macc 6:22, 27, 29, 39)

Reflection: After the priest Eleazar completed his prayer for God's mercy (see above), God took charge of the event about to take place with the Jews in the hippodrome and the drunk elephants; he caused confusion, bound the enemy with invisible shackles, and turned the stampeding elephants around so that they destroyed the king's forces. Then, according to the author of this (OT) A Third Book of Maccabees, he turned King Philopater's anger to pity, as noted in the above Scripture passage. The One with the power to save the nation of Israel, went a step further. He caused the king to issue orders to unfetter the Jews and send them home. He proclaims a seven-day festival, complete with wine and anything else needed (3 Macc 6:30). The Jews formed a choral group to accompany the festivities with thanksgiving and psalms (3 Macc 6:35). The narrator notes that it was the Lord who revealed his mercy and rescued the Jews, as noted in the passage above.

There is no doubt that this third (3 Macc 2:25—6:41) of three episodes in the Third Book of Maccabees is designed to emphasize the role of divine providence in the lives of Jews living in Egypt. In biblical numerology, three is the number for God (not Trinity). When the number three is used, it indicates the divine presence. Thus, in the account of the Jews arrested and placed in the hippodrome, they are about to be killed three times, and, of course, God saves them every time. Furthermore, the narrator states that they were to be destroyed on the fifth to the seventh of Epeiph (July 7—August 15), "the three days on which the Lord of all most gloriously revealed his mercy and rescued them all together and unharmed" (3 Macc 6:38-39). In a letter that concludes the Third Book of Maccabees, Philopater declares "the great God guiding [his] affairs" (3 Macc 7:2), states that he has "come to realize that the God of heaven surely defends the Jews, always taking their part as a father does for his children" (3 Macc 7:6), and that should he devised any evil against the Jews or cause them any grief at all, he will not have a mortal "but the Ruler over every power, the Most High God, in everything and inescapably as an antagonist to avenge such acts" (3 Macc 7:9). Thus, three times he acknowledges God. Finally, so as not to leave any doubt that God's mercy was revealed, in the last lines of the book the narrator states: "So the supreme God perfectly performed great deeds for their deliverance. Blessed be the Deliverer of Israel through all times. Amen" (3 Macc 7:22b-23).

Psalm Response: "... [Y]ou, GOD, shield me on all sides; / You ground my feet, you lift my head high; / With all my might I shout up to GOD, / His answers thunder from the holy mountain. / Real help comes from GOD, / Your blessing clothes your people! (Ps 3:3–4, 8)

Meditation/Journal: When has God revealed his mercy to you? Where did the biblical number three appear?

Prayer: Most High God, in the past you performed great deeds to rescue your people from their enemies. Manifest your mercy in my life by doing great deeds and making me aware of your divine presence. May you, Deliverer of Israel, be blessed today, tomorrow, and forever. Amen.

Asking for Mercy 2

Scripture: "Thus says the Lord: I brought this people out of bondage, and I gave them commandments through my servants the prophets; but they would not listen to them, and made my counsels void. The mother who bore them says to them, 'Go, my children, because I am a widow and forsaken. I brought you up with gladness; but with mourning and sorrow I have lost you, because you have sinned before the Lord God and have done what is evil in my sight. But now what can I do for you? For I am a widow and forsaken. Go, my children, and ask for mercy from the Lord.'" (2 Esd 2:1–4)

Reflection: The OT (A) book of Second Esdras is a composite book; it contains three works of different origins. The only group that considers it canonical is the Armenian Church; it is not found in either Catholic or Protestant Bibles. Nevertheless, it presents several passages about God's mercy. The passage above comes from a series of the Lord's oracles in which Ezra is called by God to denounce the people of Israel for their sins and to remind them of all the mercy God has showed them. Earlier in the book, God states, "I will turn to other nations and will give them my name, so that they may keep my statutes. Because you have forsaken me, I also will forsake you. When you beg mercy of me, I will show you no mercy" (2 Esd 1:24b–25). In another oracle, the Lord Almighty states, "... [Y]ou should be my people and I should be your God, and ... you should be my children and I should be your father. I will cast you out from my presence" (2 Esd 1:29, 30c). In other words, God thinks that he has done everything to preserve the covenant.

Apocrypha/Deuterocanonicals

In the passage above, God recounts some of what he did for his people. He led them out of Egyptian slavery and gave them his Torah through his prophets, but they would not listen. The mother who gave birth to them is Jerusalem, who is personified. She considers herself a widow, forsaken by God. The gladness she once had with God's presence has turned to mourning and sorrow because her children (the Jews) have sinned. Now, all they can do is ask for mercy from the Lord. Jerusalem's children are "scattered among the nations" (2 Esd 2:7); the Northern Kingdom of Israel was conquered by the Assyrians; the Southern Kingdom of Judah was conquered by the Babylonians. This part of Second Esdras (1:4—2:41) comes from a Christian community which is separating itself from its mother, Judaism. This becomes clear in another oracle in which the Lord states that he intended Jerusalem for Israel, but now he is giving it to Christians (2 Esd 2:10). "Mother, embrace your children [the church]; bring them up with gladness, as does a dove; strengthen their feet, because I have chosen you, says the Lord" (2 Esd 2:15). The author of this book presents an interpretation of the destruction of the Second Temple by the Romans in 70 CE. God left Jerusalem (a Jewish widow with children), but he has embraced another mother (a Christian with children). Needless to say, Paul disagrees with this author in his CB (NT) Letter to the Romans: He asks his readers if God has rejected his people? He answer by saying that he has not (Rom 11:1ab). It seems like the author of this part of Second Esdras did not think critically about what he was recording. As Paul states, God has not rejected his people (Rom 11:2); their stumbling has brought salvation to the Gentiles. In other words, Israel's refusal has enabled Gentile obedience to God (Rom 11:11–12). And the Gentiles didn't have to ask for that mercy; God chose to show it to them (Rom 11:13–14).

Psalm Response: "Good people, cheer GOD! / Right-living people sound best when praising. / For GOD's Word is solid to the core; / everything he makes is sound inside and out. / He loves it when everything fits, / when his world is in plumb-line true. / Earth is drenched / in GOD's affectionate satisfaction. / Blessed is the country with GOD for God; / blessed are the people he's put in his will." (Ps 33:1, 4–5, 12)

Meditation/Journal: When have you denounced someone (or a group of people) only to realize that you were excluding someone (or a group of people) from humanity (Adam's brood)? When did you realize that God was bestowing mercy on you?

Prayer: Almighty God, you create every human being in your image and likeness, and you fill them with your spirit. Help me to recognize in others the spirit that binds us together with you. Give me the courage to include rather than exclude. Hear this request for mercy today, tomorrow, and forever. Amen.

Proclaim Mercy 1

Scripture: "Rejoice, O mother, with your children, because I will deliver you, says the Lord. Remember your children that sleep, because I will bring them out of the hiding places of the earth, and will show mercy to them; for I am merciful, says the Lord Almighty. Embrace your children until I come, and proclaim mercy to them, because my springs run over, and my grace will not fail." (2 Esd 2:30–32)

Reflection: As already noted above, the OT (A) book of Second Esdras is a composite book; it contains three works of different origins. It presents several passages about God's mercy. The passage above, part of Second Esdras (1:4—2:41), comes from a Christian community which is separating itself from its mother, Judaism. This becomes clear in another oracle in which the Lord states that he intended Jerusalem for Israel, but now he is giving it to Christians (2 Esd 2:10). He exhorts the Christian mother with her children to rejoice because he will protect and deliver them, just like he once delivered the Hebrews from Egyptian slavery and the Jews from Babylonian captivity. ". . . [W]hen the day of tribulation and anguish comes, . . . you shall rejoice and have abundance," states the Lord (2 Esd 2:27). "My power will protect you, so that your children may not see hell," says the Lord (2 Esd 2:29). He also promises to raise the dead members of the church and, in so doing, show mercy to them. On the day of judgment, Second Esdras declares that God will have mercy on both living and dead Christians.

In his First Letter to the Thessalonians in the CB (NT), Paul writes similar sentiments. According to the apostle, "since we believe that Jesus died and rose again, . . . through Jesus, God will bring with him those who have died" (1 Thess 4:14). Those "who are alive, who are left until the coming of the Lord, will by no means precede those who have died" (1 Thess 4:15). Paul declares that the Lord himself will descend from heaven, raise the dead, and gather those still living to be with the Lord forever (1 Thess 4:16–17). Paul, like the author of the section of Second Esdras above, understands his words to offer encouragement to those who think the end of the world is imminent. For thousands of years, people have waited for the world to end! Such a presupposition is grounded in the daily experiences of the beginning and end of things. What is not considered in that limited view is the possibility that the world is without end. The proclamation of God's mercy includes the promise that the springs of his grace and mercy overflow and never go dry.

Psalm Response: "GOD claims Earth and everything in it. / GOD claims World and all who live on it. / He built it on Ocean foundations, / laid it out on River girders. / Who can climb Mount GOD? / Who can scale the holy north-face? / Only the clean-handed, / only the pure-hearted; / Men who won't cheat, / women who won't seduce. / GOD is at their side; / with GOD's help they make it. This . . . is what happens / to God-seekers, God-questers." (Ps 24:1–4)

Meditation/Journal: When have you experienced the Lord's merciful protection? From what did God deliver you? Do you think the world will end? Explain.

Prayer: When I need protection, give me to drink of the springs of your grace and mercy, Lord Almighty. And grant that what I experience now may be but a taste of the life you bestow upon me after you deliver me from the grave. Amen.

Worthy of Mercy

Scripture: ". . . I [, Ezra,] answered [Uriel] and said, 'I implore you, my lord, why have I been endowed with the power of understanding? For I did not wish to inquire about the ways above, but about those things that we daily experience; why Israel has been given over to the Gentiles in disgrace; why the people whom you loved has been given over to godless tribes, and the law of our ancestors has been brought to destruction and the written covenants no longer exist. We pass from the world like locusts, and our life is like a mist, and we are not worthy to obtain mercy." (2 Esd 4:22–24)

Reflection: The passage above comes from the second of three works contained in the OT (A) composite book known as Second Esdras. The second work (Esdras 3:1—14:48) is divided into seven episodes or visions.

The above passage comes from the first episode (2 Esd 3:1–5:20) in which Ezra dialogues with Uriel, "the angel that had been sent to [him]" (2 Esd 4:1). Before the angel arrives, Ezra laments the destruction of Jerusalem in 587 BCE by the Babylonian force (2 Esd 3:4–36). Ezra admits that the inhabitants of the city transgressed the law, and so God handed it over to his enemies (2 Esd 3:25–27). Now, Ezra is attempting to comprehend the way of the Most High, and the angel Uriel, whose name means *God is my flame*, appears to Ezra to dialogue with him. It is important not to conceive of the angel as a winged person; the meaning of his name gives away his identity. He is God in disguise, like Moses' experience of God as a flame of fire out of a bush (Exod 3:3).

Uriel (God) begins his conversation with Ezra by stating: "Go, weigh for me the weight of fire, or measure for me a blast of wind, or call back for me the day that is past" (2 Esd 4:5). Even though Ezra experiences fire, wind, and day, he cannot do what Uriel wants him to do. Just as Ezra cannot understand those things, so he cannot comprehend the way of the Most High (2 Esd 4:11). Thus, Uriel draws a firm line between human knowledge and divine knowledge. That doesn't stop Ezra from asking the angel why he has been endowed with the power of understanding, yet he cannot understand why God let Jerusalem be destroyed. Ezra compares a human lifetime to a locust's lifetime, eight to ten weeks! He also compares it to the morning fog, which lasts only a short time until the sun evaporates it. He concludes that because a human lifetime is so short, people are not worthy to obtain the mercy of understanding why Jerusalem was destroyed and the Jews exiled. However, as the angel tells Ezra, in the future world, perfect and eternal, all will be made right; in the future, people will be worthy of mercy.

Psalm Response: "O sovereign Lord, . . . Are the deeds of those who inhabit Babylon any better? Is that why it has gained dominion over Zion? For when I came here I saw ungodly deeds without number, and my soul has seen many sinners during these thirty years. And my heart failed me, because I have seen how you endure those who sin, and have spared those who act wickedly, and have destroyed your people, and protected your enemies, and have not shown to anyone how your way may be comprehended. Are the deeds of Babylon better than those of Zion? Or has another nation known you besides Israel?" (NRSV, 2 Esd 3:4, 28–32a)

Meditation/Journal: When have you not received God's mercy? What questions did you ask?

Prayer: Most High, I cannot weigh fire, measure a blast of wind, or call back yesterday. I cannot understand your ways, but I trust your promise and place my hope in your future. Send the flame of your Spirit to guide me in all my deeds today, tomorrow, and forever. Amen.

Not Able to Have Mercy

Scripture: "[Uriel] answered [Ezra] and said, 'This present world is not the end; the full glory does not remain in it; therefore those who were strong prayed for the weak. But the day of judgment will be the end of this age and the beginning of the immortal age to come, in which corruption has passed away, sinful indulgence has come to an end, unbelief has been cut off, and righteousness has increased and truth has appeared. Therefore no one will then be able to have mercy on someone who has been condemned in the judgment, or to harm someone who is victorious.'" (2 Esd 7:112–115)

Reflection: The passage above comes from the second of three works contained in the OT (A) composite book known as Second Esdras. The second work (Esdras 3:1—14:48) is divided into seven episodes or visions. The above passage comes from the third episode (2 Esd 6:36—9:26) in which Ezra dialogues with Uriel, "the angel that had been sent to [him]" (2 Esd 7:1). In one dialogue session, Uriel tells Ezra that the living pass through difficult and futile experiences to receive what God has reserved for them (2 Esd 7:14). In other words, there are obstacles in this world to reaching the world to come. Uriel has in mind Israel's suffering in exile. However, he shifts the conversation to a broader perspective, stating, "The righteous ... can endure difficult circumstances while hoping for easier ones; but those who have done wickedly have suffered the difficult circumstances and will never see the easier ones" (2 Esd 7:18). Throughout the dialogue, Uriel maintains that God's law is binding on all humanity, and people get what they deserve. This leads to the next dialogue about judgement, for which Uriel presents a step-by-step process to Ezra (2 Esd 7:26-44). Ultimately, Ezra asks Uriel if "on the day of judgment the righteous will be able to intercede for the ungodly or to entreat the Most High for them" (2 Esd 7:102). Uriel answers that "no one shall ever pray for another on that day ... for ... all shall bear their own righteousness and unrighteousness" (2 Esd 7:105). In other words, Uriel insists on individual responsibility for salvation. And that brings us to the passage above.

Uriel reminds Ezra that the present world is not all there is. The world to come is full of divine glory, and, therefore, it is not for sinners. In the present world, the strong in faith prayed for the weak, but when this world ends and judgment takes place, no one will be able to show mercy to another. For Uriel, who represents the perspective of the author, the day of judgment represents the end of the present world and the beginning of the eternal one where corruption, indulgence, and unbelief are gone. Only righteousness and truth remain. Thus, no opportunity to show mercy exists for someone condemned in the judgment. For this author, mercy exists only in the present world; there is no mercy in the next world; one is not able to show mercy in the next world.

Psalm Response: Ezra prayed: ". . . O Lord, you spoke at the beginning of creation . . . . On the sixth day you commanded the earth to bring forth before you cattle, wild animals, and creeping things; and over these you placed Adam, as ruler over all the works that you had made; and from him we have all come, the people whom you have chosen. All this I have spoken before you, O Lord, because you have said that it was for us that you created this world. . . . [W]e your people, whom you have called your firstborn, only begotten, zealous for you, and most dear, have been given into [other nations'] hands. If the world has indeed been created for us, why do we not possess our world as an inheritance? How long will this be so?" (NRSV, 2 Esd 6:38, 53–55, 58–59)

Meditation/Journal: For you, what is the purpose of passing through difficult and futile experiences? Do you think the present world will end? Explain. According to the author of Second Esdras, why is it important to show mercy in the present world? How would you answer Ezra's two questions that end his prayer (Psalm Response) above?

Prayer: Most High God, only with your grace can I live a holy and righteous life in the present world. Grant me an abundance of your life here and now that I may merit a full share in your glory in the world to come. Hear my prayer today, tomorrow, and for the rest of my life in this present world. Amen.

Apocrypha/Deuterocanonicals

Merciful

Scripture: "[Ezra] answered [Uriel] and said, 'I know, O Lord, that the Most High is now called merciful, because he has mercy on those who have not yet come into the world; and gracious because he is gracious to those who turn in repentance to his law; and patient, because he shows patience toward those who have sinned, since they are his own creatures; and bountiful, because he would rather give than take away; and abundant in compassion, because he makes his compassion abound more and more to those now living and to those who are gone and to those yet to come—for if he did not make them abound, the world with those who inhabit it would not have life—and he is called the giver, because if he did not give out of his goodness so that those who have committed iniquities might be relived of them not one-ten-thousandth of humankind would have life; and the judge, because if he did not pardon those who were created by his word and blot out the multitude of their sins, there would probably be left only very few of the innumerable multitude.'" (2 Esd 7:132–140)

Reflection: The passage above comes from the second of three works contained in the OT (A) composite book known as Second Esdras. The second work (Esdras 3:1—14:48) is divided into seven episodes or visions. The above passage comes from the third episode (2 Esd 6:36—9:26) in which Ezra dialogues with Uriel, "the angel that had been sent to [him]" (2 Esd 7:1). Uriel tells Ezra that for those who choose life, as Moses instructed, there will be joy over their assured salvation. This leads Ezra to respond with the above passage, which is a commentary on the HB (OT) book of Exodus 34:6–7: "The LORD, the LORD, / a God merciful and gracious, / slow to anger, / and abounding in steadfast love and faithfulness, / keeping steadfast love for the thousandth generation, / forgiving iniquity and transgression and sin, / yet by no means clearing the guilty . . . ." Ezra declares that the LORD is named Merciful, because he has pity on those not yet born by bringing them to birth (see Psalm Response below). He is gracious, sharing himself with those who repent; he is patient, because he endures waiting for sinners, whom he created. God is generous, giving rather than taking, overflowing in compassion to those of the past, present, and future. Without his abundance there would be no life. God's nature is to give out of his goodness to such a degree that he overwhelms iniquities. But God is also the judge, who pardons sins. In other words, if God were not merciful, there would be very few people alive.

Uriel responds to Ezra's commentary by stating that God made the world for the sake of the many, but the world to come he made for the sake of the few (2 Esd 8:1). Uriel reinforces his point by telling Ezra a parable: "... [W]hen you ask the earth, it will tell you that it provides a large amount of clay from which earthenware is made, but only a little dust from which gold comes, so is the course of the present world. Many have been created, but only a few shall be saved" (2 Esd 8:2-3). In a similar vein, the CB (NT) Matthean Jesus warns his disciples against complacency and misplaced security in his Sermon on the Mount, stating: "Enter through the narrow gate; for the gate is wide and the road is easy that leads to destruction, and there are many who take it. For the gate is narrow and the road is hard that leads to life, and there are few who find it" (Matt 7:13-14). Likewise, the Lukan Jesus answers a question about only a few being saved by teaching, "Strive to enter through the narrow door; for many, I tell you will try to enter and will not be able" (Luke 13:24). Ezra finds that God is merciful, even though Uriel and Jesus place more emphasis on God's justice!

Psalm Response: "O Lord above us, grant to your servant that we may pray before you, and give us a seed for our heart and cultivation of our understanding so that fruit may be produced, by which every mortal who bears the likeness of a human being may be able to live. For you alone exist, and we are a work of your hands as you have declared. And because you give life to the body that is now fashioned in the womb, and furnish it with members, what you have created is preserved amid fire and water, and for nine months the womb endures your creature that has been created in it. But that which keeps and that which is kept shall both be kept by your keeping. And when the womb gives up again what has been created in it, you have commanded that from the members themselves ... milk ... should be supplied, so that what has been fashioned may be nourished for a time; and afterwards you will still guide it in your mercy." (NRSV, 2 Esd 8:6-11)

Meditation/Journal: On what side do you find yourself: Uriel and Jesus (justice)—only a few saved—or Ezra (mercy)—many saved? Do you think humankind exists because of God's mercy (as illustrated in the Psalm Response above) or because parents desire an heir? Explain.

Prayer: Hear, O Lord, the prayer of your servant. Have pity on me. Mercifully forgive me my sins, and bestow the grace of righteousness upon me.

Then, I will praise your righteousness and goodness and declare that you are merciful to all your creatures forever. Amen.

Mercy on Inheritance?

Scripture: "[Ezra] answered [Uriel] and said, 'If I have found favor in your sight, let me speak. If the farmer's seed does not come up, because it has not received your rain in due season, or if it has been ruined by too much rain, it perishes. But people, who have been formed by your hands and are called your own image because they are made like you, and for whose sake you have formed all things—have you also made them like the farmer's seed? Surely not, O Lord above! But spare your people and have mercy on your inheritance, for you have mercy on your own creation.'" (2 Esd 8:42–45)

Reflection: The passage above comes from the second of three works contained in the OT (A) composite book known as Second Esdras. The second work (Esdras 3:1—14:48) is divided into seven episodes or visions. The above passage comes from the third episode (2 Esd 6:36—9:26) in which Ezra dialogues with Uriel, "the angel that had been sent to [him]" (2 Esd 7:1). Uriel, whose name means *God is my flame*, presents an analogy to Ezra: ". . . [J]ust as the farmer sows many seeds in the ground, and plants a multitude of seedlings, and yet not all that have been sown will come up in due season, and not all that were planted will take root; so also those who have been sown in the world will not all be saved" (2 Esd 8:41). Uriel is focused on the responsibility for salvation on the individual. Ezra knows that Uriel is God in disguise, and he presents the weakness in the analogy, stating that if the seed does not grow, it may be because it didn't receive enough rain or it received too much rain. Then, addressing Uriel directly as God, Ezra reminds the divine that he made people in his image; thus, people are not like the farmer's seed. In other words, Ezra presents what he considers to be a biblical view. Every person is created in God's likeness, and every person deserves to be spared. God needs to show mercy to his people, his inheritance, his own creatures. Basically, Ezra argues that God is interested in showing mercy to sinners!

Uriel (God) replies to Ezra, stating, ". . . [Y]ou come far short of being able to love my creation more than I love it" (2 Esd 8:47). Uriel (God) explains that God does not will that anything he created perishes. People have the opportunity to choose (2 Esd 8:56). God does not intend that anyone be destroyed (2 Esd 8:59). God is not to blame for the destruction of human beings, who choose their own fate (2 Esd 7:72, 129–131). Uriel (God) is very clear that all people received God's benefits, but they did not acknowledge him; they scorned his law even while they enjoyed their freedom; they did not take advantage of their opportunities for repentance (2 Esd 9:10–11). "I considered my world, and saw that it was lost," states Uriel (God) (2 Esd 9:20a). Thus, only a remnant will be saved. In the CB (NT), Paul tells the Romans, ". . . Christ is the end of the law so that there may be righteousness for everyone who believes" (Rom 10:4). The apostle does not think that the law can save; only God can save, and that is what he did in Christ Jesus. "There is . . . no condemnation for those who are in Christ Jesus," writes Paul. "For the law of the Spirit of life in Christ Jesus has set you free from the law of sin and of death. For God has done what the law, weakened by the flesh, could not do; by sending his own Son in the likeness of sinful flesh, and to deal with sin, he condemned sin in the flesh, so that the just requirement of the law might be fulfilled in us, who walk not according to the flesh but according to the Spirit" (Rom 8:1–5). In his letter to the Romans, Paul presents what he considers to be God's plan to save both Jews and Gentiles (Rom 9:1—11:36).

Psalm Response: "O Lord, you showed yourself among us, to our ancestors in the wilderness when they came out from Egypt and when they came into the untrodden and unfruitful wilderness; and you said, 'Hear me, O Israel, and give heed to my words, O descendants of Jacob. For I sow my law in you, and it shall bring forth fruit in you, and you shall be glorified through it forever.' But though our ancestors received the law, they did not keep it and did not observe the statutes; yet the fruit of the law did not perish—for it could not, because it was yours. Yet those who received it perished, because they did not keep what had been sown in them." (NRSV, 2 Esd 9:29–33)

Meditation/Journal: Do you think all will be saved, like Ezra; that only a few will be saved, like Uriel; or that God has a plan to save all in Christ Jesus, like Paul? Explain. Which perspective best illustrates God's mercy?

Prayer: O Lord, you spare your people, and you have mercy on your inheritance, for you have mercy on your own creation. Bestow upon me that mercy that I may grow in understanding of your ways and be saved by you, who are always merciful. Hear my petition today and tomorrow. Amen.

Apocrypha/Deuterocanonicals

Set Free in Mercy

Scripture: "... [A]s for the lion whom you saw [in your dream] rousing up out of the forest and roaring and speaking to the eagle and reproving him for his unrighteousness, and as for all his words that you have heard, this is the Messiah whom the Most High has kept until the end of days, who will arise from the offspring of David, and will come and speak with them. He will denounce them for their ungodliness and for their wickedness, and will display before them their contemptuous dealings. For first he will bring them alive before his judgment seat, and when he has reproved them, then he will destroy them. But in mercy he will set free the remnant of my people, those who have been saved throughout my borders, and he will make them joyful until the end comes, the day of judgment...." (2 Esd 12:31–34)

Reflection: The passage above comes from the second of three works contained in the OT (A) composite book known as Second Esdras. The second work (Esdras 3:1—14:48) is divided into seven episodes or visions written around 100 CE. The above passage comes from the fifth episode (2 Esd 11:1—12:54) in which Ezra has a dream about an eagle and a lion. The apocalyptic nature of the book comes through most visibly in Ezra's apocalyptic dream; he, a human, receives revelations and interpretations concerning the divine plan of history and the supernatural world. The voice of the angel Uriel, who has been present as dialogue partner in the previous four episodes, disappears and is replaced with a voice (2 Esd 11:36) that interprets the scribe's dream. The eagle represents the Roman Empire, which, at the end of time, according to this book, will be destroyed (2 Esd 12:3). The lion represents the anointed one (Messiah), whom God has kept until the last day and will send to judge the Roman Empire (which existed at the time this book was written) for its harsh treatment of the Jews. He will set free the Jews he will save as a demonstration of his mercy.

Christian readers are cautioned not to jump to conclusions about the Messiah being Jesus, even though the judgment scene in Second Esdras is like that found in the CB (NT) Gospel of Matthew (25: 31–46). Messiah is the Hebrew word for *anointed one*, just like Christ is the Greek word for *anointed one*. The author of Second Esdras notes that the anointed one will arise from the offspring of David. In the HB (OT), the book of Genesis records Jacob's last words to his sons; among those are these: "Judah is a lion's whelp; / from the prey, my son, you have gone up" (Gen 49:9a). These words anticipate the preeminence and prosperity of the royal line of King

David, who arose out of the tribe of Judah. "He crouches down, he stretches out like a lion, / like a lioness—who dares rouse him up?" (Gen 49:9b) The same imagery is at work in the CB (NT) book of Revelation, in which the slaughtered lamb is identified as "the Lion of the tribe of Judah, the Root of David" (Rev 5:5b). Throughout Second Esdras, Ezra's concern has been for the salvation of the Jews; he has sought divine mercy. The voice—the interpreter of his dream—tells him: "... [T]hose who are left of your people, who are found within my holy borders, shall be saved. Therefore when [the Messiah] destroys the multitude of the nations that are gathered, he will defend the people who remain" (2 Esd 13:48-49). Those who have remained faithful will be set free in mercy.

Psalm Response: "O sovereign Lord, if I have found favor in your sight, and if I have been accounted righteous before you beyond many others, and if my prayer has indeed come up before your face, strengthen me and show me, your servant, the interpretation and meaning of this terrifying vision so that you may fully comfort my soul." (NRSV, 2 Esd 12:7-8)

Meditation/Journal: Who (or What) is your anointed one? In mercy, from what have you been set free? Explain.

Prayer: Most High, through patriarchs and matriarchs, judges, kings, and prophets, you have revealed your mercy. Send your Spirit to guide me in your ways and to fill me with your wisdom. Set me free in mercy to serve you today, tomorrow, and forever. Amen.

Merciful Afterlife

Scripture: "Hear these words, O Israel. If you then, will rule over your minds and discipline your hearts, you shall be kept alive, and after death you shall obtain mercy. For after death the judgment will come when we shall live again; then the names of the righteous shall become manifest, and the deeds of the ungodly shall be disclosed." (2 Esd 14:28, 34-35)

Reflection: The passage above comes from the second of three works contained in the OT (A) composite book known as Second Esdras. The second work (Esdras 3:1—14:48) is divided into seven episodes or visions. The above passage comes from the seventh episode (2 Esd 14:1—48). The episode begins with Ezra sitting under an oak tree (2 Esd 14:1)—evoking

Apocrypha/Deuterocanonicals

scenes of Abraham sitting under the oaks of Mamre (Gen 18:1) and Gideon under the oak at Ophrah (Judg 6:11)—and hearing a voice coming from a bush—evoking the scene of Moses on Mount Horeb (Sinai) (Exod 3:4). There can be doubt that it is the Lord speaking: the number three, a code for God, is present (2 Esd 14:1); Ezra answers the voice using Isaiah's words (Isa 6:8), "Here I am, Lord" (2 Esd 14:2); and God says, "I revealed myself in a bush and spoke to Moses when my people were in bondage in Egypt" (2 Esd 14:3). Then, God tells Ezra that he intends to take him up from humankind (2 Esd 14:9)—evoking Enoch (Gen 5:24)—but Ezra says, "if then I have found favor with you, send the holy spirit into me, and I will write everything that has happened in the world from the beginning, the things that were written in your law, so that people may be able to find the path, and that those who want to live in the last days may do so" (2 Esd 14:22).

Then, before he begins to write, he speaks to his people, the Israelites. He reminds them that they witnessed God's mercy when they were liberated from Egyptian slavery. At Horeb (Sinai) God gave them the law, a way of life, which they did not keep. They traveled to the land promised to Abraham and his descendants, but the Israelites did not obey the way of life of the Most High, who let them be destroyed and exiled by Assyria and Babylon. Ezra urges them to discipline their minds and hearts to receive life (mercy) after death and judgment. Then, after drinking water the color of fire (2 Esd 14:39), a code for inspiration, Ezra begins to write.

Psalm Response: "GOD looks after us all, / makes us robust with life— / Lucky to be in the land, / we're free from enemy worries. / Whenever we're sick and in bed, / GOD becomes our nurse, / nurses us back to health. / GOD, give grace, get me up on my feet. / You know me inside and out, you hold me together, / you never fail to stand me tall in your presence / so I can look you in the eye. / Blessed is GOD, Israel's God, / always, always, always. / Yes. Yes. Yes." (Ps 41:2–4, 12–13)

Meditation/Journal: Do you think there is judgment after death followed by an afterlife? What is the basis for your understanding? Do you consider an afterlife a revelation of God's mercy? Explain.

Prayer: Most High God, you light the lamp of understanding in the hearts of people. With the fire of your Spirit ignite the light within me, that I may know your will and strive to do it. If you have found favor with me, hear this prayer today, tomorrow, and forever. Amen.

Psalm 136:1

3

Christian Bible (New Testament)

Gospels

Mercy in Kind

Scripture: "... [T]he kingdom of heaven may be compared to a king who wished to settle accounts with his slaves.... [O]ne owed him ten thousand talents.... [T]he slave fell on his knees... And out of pity for him, the lord of that slave... forgave him the debt. But that same slave, as he went out, came upon one of his fellow slaves who owed him a hundred denarii.... [H]is fellow slave fell down and pleaded with him.... But he refused; then he went and threw him into prison until he would pay the debt. Then his lord summoned him and said to him, 'You wicked slave! I forgave you all that debt because you pleaded with me. Should you not have had mercy on your fellow slave, as I had mercy on you?'" (Matt 18:23–24, 26–29, 32–33)

Reflection: In the CB (NT) Gospel according to Matthew, the unique parable of the unforgiving servant, from which the above passage is taken, there is presented a lesson about both divine mercy and human mercy. Divine mercy is found in the king, who is compared to the "heavenly Father" (Matt 18:35). In the parable, the king, who owns slaves, decides to settle or square (Peterson) accounts with slaves who owe him money. One slave owes his master ten thousand talents. In the ancient world, a talent was worth more than fifteen years' total wages paid to a laborer! Thus, this slave

Christian Bible (New Testament)

owes 150,000 year's wages! In one lifetime, he would not be able to pay it, and his master shows him pity (mercy) by forgiving him the debt! According to the parable, this is how God treats people; he shows them mercy by forgiving them unlimitedly! In other words, what people are unable to give to God, God gives to them.

The slave, whose debt is canceled by the king, is owed a hundred denarii by one of his fellow slaves. The usual daily wage for a laborer was a denarius. Thus, the slave's fellow slave owes him one hundred days' wages, an amount that could be repaid. However, when his fellow slave seeks mercy, he refuses to give it. When the master of both slaves hears what he did, he summons him to his chamber and asks him one question, according to Peterson: "Shouldn't you be compelled to be merciful to your fellow servant who asked for mercy?" (Matt 18:33) NAB asks: "Should you not have had pity on your fellow servant, as I had pity on you?" (Matt 18:33) CEV presents the question in a wider dimension: "Do you think you should show pity to someone else, as I did to you?" (Matt 18:33) The question is not answered in the parable; the reader must give an answer for the second slave. The inevitable answer of "Yes" implies that divine, extravagant mercy should be passed on in kind to fellow human beings. In other words, just as the human debt to God is unpayable, so is the human debt unpayable to a fellow human being. All that a person can do is give mercy in kind.

Psalm Response: "God of my ancestors, Lord of my mercies! When you spoke, all creation broke loose. After consulting Lady Wisdom you appointed humankind to ride herd on the creatures you'd made and to manage the world with commitment and justice, erring more on the side of the heart than the mind. Grant me access to Lady Wisdom, and count me as one of your children." (Wis 9:1–4)

Meditation/Journal: How do you answer the question: Should you not have mercy on others, as God has mercy on you? What are the implications (or consequences) in your answer? Explain.

Prayer: Heavenly Father, through the parable told by your Son, Jesus, you teach about your extravagant gift of mercy that you intend be shared with others. Fill my heart with understanding and appreciation for your gift, and give me the courage to show pity to those around me by sharing the mercy I receive from you. Send me your help today, tomorrow, and forever. Amen.

Proclaim Mercy 2

Scripture: Jesus and the twelve "came to the other side of the sea, to the country of the Gerasenes. And when he had stepped out of the boat, immediately a man out of the tombs with an unclean spirit met him. He lived among the tombs; and no one could restrain him any more.... When he saw Jesus from a distance, he ran and bowed down before him.... And the unclean spirits came out.... [T]he man who had been possessed by demons begged [Jesus] that he might be with him. But Jesus refused and said to him, 'Go home to your friends and tell them how much the Lord has done for you, and what mercy he has shown you.'" (Mark 5:1–3, 6a, 13b, 17b–19)

Reflection: The source for the above narrative is the CB (NT) Gospel according to Mark (5:1–20). Other versions of the story are found in the derivative gospels of Matthew (8:28–34), in which it is the country of the Gadarenes, and Luke (8:26–39), in which it is the country of the Gerasenes. The narrative in Mark's Gospel features themes that are characteristic of the unknown author. First, the author of Mark's Gospel likes to tell stories about demons, understood to refer to any kind of illness affecting people. The man in Mark's story lives among tombs; he is "dead," an outcast in his society. Throughout Mark's Gospel demons always know who Jesus is, whereas disciples do not! Such is the case here; the man calls him "Jesus, Son of the Most High God" (Mark 5:7). As the Markan Jesus always does, he drives out the demons; in this account they enter swine—unclean animals forbidden to Jews—and rush down a bank into the sea, where they drown!

The man wants to join Jesus' gang, but the Markan Jesus, who usually tells people to maintain secrecy about him, tells this man to go home to his friends, or his own people (Peterson) or to his family (NAB, CEV) and, uncharacteristically of the Markan Jesus, tell what mercy the Lord has showed him. In other words, the Markan Jesus mandates a proclamation of divine mercy. While many readers will not recognize the man "sitting there, clothed and in his right mind" (Mark 5:15), he reappears at the end of Mark's Gospel. The women who go to Jesus' tomb—it is important to note the similarity of place—discover "a young man, dressed in a white robe, sitting on the right side" (Mark 16:5). Not only is the young man clothed, but he tells the women, "... [G]o, tell his disciples ...." (Mark 16:7). In other words, what he was once told to do—to proclaim mercy—he now sends the spice-bearing women to do the same. Divine mercy needs to be proclaimed.

Psalm Response: "... [B]less the God of all, / who everywhere works great wonders, / who fosters our growth from birth, / and deals with us according to his mercy. / May he give us gladness of heart, / and may there be peace in our days / in Israel, as in the days of old. / May he entrust to us his mercy, / and may he deliver us in our days!" (NRSV, Sir 50:22-24)

Meditation/Journal: What do you consider to be modern demons from which people need to be healed? Explain. Where have you proclaimed God's mercy? For what did you proclaim mercy?

Prayer: Every day, O Lord, finds you healing your people, who proclaim your abundant mercy. Your benignancy to me from my birth knows no bounds. Fill me with your Spirit, and send me to proclaim your mercy today, tomorrow, and forever. Amen.

Samaritan Mercy

Scripture: "A man was going down from Jerusalem to Jericho, and fell into the hands of robbers, who stripped him, beat him, and went away, leaving him half dead.... [A] Samaritan while traveling came near him; and when he saw him, he was moved with pity. He went to him and bandaged his wounds, having poured oil and wine on them. [Jesus asked a lawyer:] ... [W]as [he] a neighbor to the man who fell into the hands of the robbers?' [The lawyer said,] '... [He] showed him mercy.' Jesus said to him, 'Go and do likewise.'" (Luke 10:30, 33-34, 36-37)

Reflection: The above passage is an abbreviated form of the story called the good Samaritan, a unique narrative in Luke's Gospel (10:25-37) in the CB (NT). Nowhere in the story is the Samaritan named good! The account begins with a lawyer (Peterson: religious scholar) asking Jesus about what he must do to inherit eternal life. Jesus asks him what he finds in the law, and he responds with the two great commandments about loving God and neighbor. Then, he asks Jesus to specify who his neighbor is. And Jesus obliges by telling the good Samaritan parable. The Jewish man travelling the road from Jerusalem to Jericho encounters robbers, who leave him half-dead in a ditch. At first a Jewish priest sees him, but he passes by; if he were to touch the man in the ditch and discover that he was dead, he would be unclean from touching a corpse. Then, a Levite, another religious minister, goes by; if he touches the man in the ditch, and the man is dead, he incurs ritual uncleanness, just like the priest. However, a Samaritan, who is already considered to be unclean, has nothing to lose! Not only does he touch the man in the ditch, rendering the Jew unclean through his own uncleanness, but he bandages his wounds and takes him to an inn, where, after spending the night with him, instructs the innkeeper to continue to care for him and he'll pay the bill when he comes back! For the Samaritan to keep the Jewish law about loving his neighbor, he must violate the law by touching the Jewish man in the ditch, making him unclean! To the Jews, a Samaritan was a member of a heretical and schismatic group, a mixed population, detested by Jews.

At the end of the story, the Lukan Jesus asks the lawyer which of the three—priest, Levite, Samaritan—was neighbor to the man in the ditch. And the lawyer must answer what, from his Jewish perspective, is impossible to say, "The Samaritan." In fact, he cannot even say the word *Samaritan*. He says that the one who showed mercy to the man in the ditch was neighbor. Peterson records, "The one who treated him kindly" (Luke 10:37) or "showed pity" (CEV). Now that the lawyer knows that his neighbor is his enemy, the man he detests, the man who makes his Jewish comrade unclean, the Lukan Jesus rubs salt into his wound, telling him to go and act like the Samaritan! In Jesus' world, no Jew would imitate a Samaritan; but in the story, it is the Samaritan who shows mercy to a Jew. And according to Jesus, the Samaritan's demonstration of mercy is to be imitated by Jews!

Psalm Response: "Yes, God of ours, you're persuasive but never abrasive, slow to anger yet quick to comfort when it comes to us poor sinners. Even if we sin, we're yours, knowing your great tolerance for sinners; the fact that you're counting us as friends is a compliment. To know you is to come face-to-face with justice; meeting your power first hand is the beginning of immortality. In making our decision we haven't been dazzled by a fast talker, nor fooled by a portrait artist, nor lured by a prideful statue." (Wis 15:1–4)

Meditation/Journal: Who is your neighbor-enemy? Explain. Who has been neighbor-enemy to you? How did his or her action catch you off guard?

Prayer: In your world, O God, all people are neighbors, even those most detested by some people. Broaden my view beyond my immediate neighbors so that I can see that my enemies are also my neighbors. Help me to imitate the Samaritan, who showed mercy to the Jewish man in the ditch, today, tomorrow, and forever. Amen.

CHRISTIAN BIBLE (NEW TESTAMENT)

Mercy not Available

Scripture: "There was a rich man who was dressed in purple and fine linen and who feasted sumptuously every day. And at his gate lay a poor man named Lazarus, covered with sores, who longed to satisfy his hunger with what fell from the rich man's table; even the dogs could come and lick his sores. The poor man died and was carried away by the angels to be with Abraham. The man also died and was buried. . . . [He] looked up and saw Abraham far away with Lazarus by his side. He called out, 'Father Abraham, have mercy on me, and send Lazarus to dip the tip of his finger in water and cool my tongue . . . .' But Abraham said, . . . '[B]etween you and us a great chasm has been fixed, so that those who might want to pass from here to you cannot do so, and no one can cross from there to us.'" (Luke 16:19–22, 26)

Reflection: One message delivered by the unique CB (NT) Gospel according to Luke story known as the Rich Man and Lazarus is that mercy that is available in this life is not available in the afterlife. The Lukan Jesus makes this point clearly, stating, ". . . [W]hat is prized by human beings is an abomination in the sight of God" (Luke 16:15). The non-named rich man prized expensive purple clothes (Peterson: the latest fashions), linen, and gourmet food (Peterson: conspicuous consumption). The poor man named Lazarus, meaning *God has helped*, prized none of those things; in fact he was dumped on the rich man's doorstep (Peterson), diseased, hungry, and near death. Once the poor man died, he was taken to Abraham, because he didn't prize what was an abomination to God. Once the rich man died and was buried, he looked up from the first level of a three-storied universe to the top level, where he saw Lazarus and Abraham. Upon seeing Abraham, he requested the mercy of a drop or two of water. However, Abraham informs him that the gate he did not walk through in his life on earth—the middle story of a three-storied universe—exists in the afterlife; no crossing the great chasm can be done. If the rich man had prized what God prized—taking care of the poor by walking through his gate, seeing Lazarus there, and clothing and feeding him—there would be no huge chasm in the afterlife. Showing mercy is an activity of the life lived on earth; after death mercy is no longer available. In other words, some of the values held by human beings in earthly life are an abomination to God in heavenly life!

This message is not one heard in a consumer-oriented culture! It is easy to fall into the practice of buying the latest fashions and expensive shoes in the local mall. One salivates when thinking about dining in the best restaurants in town. Even if the local soup kitchen, homeless shelter, food pantry, or vagrant camp is passed along the way, the car seems to keep going. As the HB (OT) makes clear, God is concerned about how the rich treat the poor (Exod 22:25; 23:3, 6, 11; Lev 14:21; 19:10, 15; 23:22; Deut 15:11; 24:12, 1415; 1 Sam 2:7–8; etc.). The poor are of particular concern in Luke's Gospel. The good news of the birth of Jesus is delivered first to the poor shepherds (Luke 2:1–20). The Lukan Jesus declares that he has been anointed "to bring good news to the poor" (Luke 4:18; 7:22). In his sermon on the plain, the Lukan Jesus begins, "Blessed are you who are poor, for yours is the kingdom of God" (Luke 6:20). He instructs his dinner party host to invite the poor (Luke 14:13, 21), a certain ruler to sell his possessions and give the money to the poor (Luke 18:22), listens to Zacchaeus tell him that he will give half his possessions to the poor (Luke 19:8), and declare a poor widow's two copper coins to be more than what the rich people put in the treasury (Luke 21:2–3). Giving to the poor, while living on the earth, where mercy is available, is better than waiting until after death, when mercy is not available.

Psalm Response: "Into the hovels of the poor, / Into the dark streets where the homeless groan, God speaks; / 'I've had enough; I'm on my way / To heal the ache in the heart of the wretched.'" (Ps 12:5)

Meditation/Journal: What opportunities exist for you to show mercy to the poor now? Make a list and choose three to five of them. Once some are chosen, use the time available for mercy.

Prayer: Biblically, Lord, your concern has always been for the poor. With your Spirit show me how I might reveal your mercy to the poor, when the opportunities for doing so are present. Then, give me the strength to do so today, tomorrow, and forever. Amen.

Letters

Mercy: Divine Choice

Scripture: "I have great sorrow and unceasing anguish in my heart . . . for my own people, my kindred according to the flesh. They are Israelites, and to them belong the adoption, the glory, the covenants, the giving of the law,

Christian Bible (New Testament)

the worship, and the promises; to them belong the patriarchs, and from then, according to the flesh, comes the Messiah, who is over all, God blessed forever. Amen. . . . [I]t is not the children of the flesh who are the children of God, but the children of the promise are counted as descendants. Is there injustice on God's part? By no means! For he says to Moses, 'I will have mercy on whom I have mercy, / and I will have compassion on whom I have compassion.' So it depends, not on human will or exertion, but on God who shows mercy. So then he has mercy on whomever he chooses . . . ." (Rom 9:2–5, 14b–16, 18)

Reflection: In the second section (9:1—11:36) of the CB (NT) Letter of Paul to the Romans, the apostle presents how he thinks God's work in Christ relates to God's purpose for the Jews and Gentiles. As can be seen in the above passage, he expresses his sorrow and anguish at the unacceptance of Jesus among the Jews. The Jews—Hebrews, Israelites—were chosen by God to be his people; to them he gave covenants and the Torah. Nevertheless, they did not accept Jesus as their Messiah. The Jews, children of the flesh, according to Paul, are not the children of God; the Gentiles are the children of the promise. According to Paul, even before they were born, God intended to elect them, not by works but by his call. There is no injustice here, as some might argue. To make his point, Paul quotes God's words in the HB (OT) book of Exodus 33:19 about him having mercy on those whom he chooses to have mercy and showing compassion to those whom he chooses to show compassion. Peterson captures those words this way: "God told Moses, '*I'm* in charge of mercy. *I'm* in charge of compassion'" (Rom 9:15). Paul concludes that God's action does not depend on human will, but on God's desire to show mercy. God has mercy on whomever he chooses. In Peterson's words: ". . . God has the first word, initiating the action in which we play our part for good or ill" (Rom 9:18).

Paul thinks that God chose to show mercy to the Gentiles "to make known the riches of his glory for the objects of mercy, which he has prepared beforehand for glory—including us whom he has called, not from the Jews only but also from the Gentiles" (Rom 9:23–24). Peterson captures Paul's conclusion: "How can we sum this up? All those people who didn't seem interested in what God was doing actually *embraced* what God was doing as he straightened out their lives. And Israel, who seemed so interested in reading and talking about what God was doing, missed it. How could they miss it? Because instead of trusting God, *they* took over. They were absorbed in what they themselves were doing. They were so absorbed

in their 'God projects' that they didn't notice God right in front of them..."
(Rom 9:30–32). In other words, the Jews got stuck in works, when God was stuck in mercy. CEV explains it this way: "Gentiles were not trying to be acceptable to God, but they found that he would accept them if they had faith.... [T]he people of Israel were not acceptable to God. And why not? It was because they were trying to be acceptable by obeying the Law instead of by having faith in God" (Rom 9:30–32). In other words, God had mercy on the Gentiles, who accepted the divine offer in faith, the capacity to trust God.

Psalm Response: "I'm thanking you, GOD, from a full heart, / I'm writing the book on your wonders. / I'm whistling, laughing, and jumping for joy; / I'm singing your song, High God." (Ps 9:1–2)

Meditation/Journal: When have you found yourself witnessing divine mercy and thinking that it was not deserved? Explain. What are the consequences if, as Paul states, God's action of showing mercy is based on his desire to show mercy? What is the role of trust of God in Pauline thought?

Prayer: LORD God, you show mercy to whom you will, and you take pity on whom you will. Show your mercy to me, and take pity on me by increasing my trust in you. Never let me think that my salvation depends on the works I do. You are over all and blessed today, tomorrow, and forever. Amen.

Receive Mercy

Scripture: "As regards the gospel [the Jews] are enemies of God for [the Gentiles'] sake; but as regards election they are beloved, for the sake of their ancestors; for the gifts and the calling of God are irrevocable. Just as you [Gentiles] were once disobedient to God but have now received mercy because of [the Jews'] disobedience, so they have now been disobedient in order that, by the mercy shown to you, they too may now receive mercy. For God has imprisoned all in disobedience so that he may be merciful to all." (Rom 11:28–32)

Reflection: In the second section (9:1—11:36) of the CB (NT) Letter of Paul to the Romans, the apostle presents how he thinks God's work in Christ relates to God's purpose for the Jews and Gentiles. After he expresses

CHRISTIAN BIBLE (NEW TESTAMENT)

his sorrow and anguish at the unacceptance of Jesus among the Jews, Paul tells the Romans that he wants them "to understand this mystery" (Rom 11:25). The mystery is that "a hardening has come upon the part of Israel, until the full number of the Gentiles has come in. And so all Israel will be saved . . ." (Rom 11:25-26). By refusing to submit to God's righteousness, a pure gift, and continuing to attempt to save themselves by adherence to Torah, the Jews have not accepted the good news that God was reconciling everyone in the world to himself in the person of Jesus the anointed. That does not imply that the Jews have been unelected; if the gifts and the call of God are revocable, then what will keep God from changing his mind about the Gentiles later? According to Paul, Peterson states: "There was a time not so long ago when you [Gentiles] were on the outs with God. But then the Jews slammed the door on him and things opened up for you. Now *they* are on the outs. But with the door held wide open for you, they have a way back in" (Rom 11:30-31). Peterson summarizes Paul's mystery this way: "In one way or another, God makes sure that we all experience what it means to be outside so that he can personally open the door and welcome us back in." Then, according to Peterson, the apostle asks: "Have you ever come on anything quite like this extravagant generosity of God, this deep, deep wisdom? It's way over our heads. We'll never figure it out" (Rom 11:33). Just as the Gentiles benefited from the Jews' bad fortune, the Jews will benefit from the Gentiles' good fortune. Such is the mystery, according to Paul, of God's work.

Paul's understanding of God's plan is that everyone has been saved. In Paul's world, one was either a Jew or a Gentile. According to Paul, the Jews' failure made it possible for the Gentiles' salvation (CEV). The Jews will become jealous of the Gentiles, and God will save them (Rom 11:11-12). Peterson refers to this as a homecoming. The Jews never lose their status as God's chosen ones; God does not take back the gifts he has given or forget about the people he has chosen, states CEV. The Gentiles have experienced divine mercy, and the Jews will experience divine mercy. Everything comes from God and will return to him. No one is able to understand why God does what he does. All anyone—Jew or Gentile—can do is stand with open hands to receive God's extravagant mercy.

Psalm Response: "My head is high, GOD, held high; / I'm looking to you, GOD; / No hangdog skulking for me. / I've thrown in my lot with you; / You won't embarrass me, will you? / Or let my enemies get the best of me? / Show me how you work, GOD; / School me in your ways. / Take me by the hand; / Lead me down the path of truth. / You are my Savior, aren't you? (Ps 25:1–3a, 4–5)

Meditation/Journal: For you, what are the consequences of Paul's statement about the Gentiles being disobedient and receiving mercy because of the Jews' disobedience? For you, what are the consequences of Paul's statement that the Gentiles' obedience will result in the Jews' reception of divine mercy? For you, what are the consequence of Paul's statement that God has imprisoned all people in disobedience so that he can be merciful to all or save all?

Prayer: Everything comes from you, God. Everything happens through you. There is no human being who can explain you; there is no human being smart enough to tell you what to do; no human being can give you a gift that is greater than the gifts you give to me. From you and through you and to you are all things. To you be glory forever. Amen.

His Mercy Endures Forever
Psalm 136:1

Lexicon

Benignancy: kind and gracious in behavior or appearance

Clemency: an instance of showing mercy or leniency; an act of mercy

Compassion: sympathy for the suffering of others

Dependable: able to be trusted to act in the way required or expected

Forbearance: patience, tolerance, self-control; refraining from doing something; refraining from legal right

Forgiveness: act of pardoning somebody for a mistake, misunderstanding, wrongdoing; cancel obligation; tendency to forgive offenses readily and easily

Generosity: kindness, willingness to give freely; nobility of character; substantial size

Grace: elegancy; generosity of spirit; gift of God to humankind; act of God sharing himself with people

Kindness: the practice of being or the capability to be sympathetic and compassionate; an act demonstrating consideration and caring

Leniency: punishment, judgment, or action that is not too severe; gentleness or tolerance; showing tolerance or mercy

Liberality: generosity; generous provision; largeness; broadmindedness; tolerance of difference views and standards of behavior

Love: intense feeling of tender affection and compassion

Lexicon

Loyally: faithful

Magnanimity: great generosity or noble spiritedness

Mercy: compassion, kindness, or forgiveness shown to an offender or to somebody a person has power over; compassionate disposition; easing of distress or pain; done from generosity, not obligation

Mildness: gentle or amiable; easy-going, slow to get angry; pleasant and temperate

Pardon: forgive somebody for wrongdoing; excuse somebody for something impolite; release from punishment; act of excusing somebody

Patience: capacity for waiting; the ability to endure waiting or delay without becoming annoyed or upset; ability to tolerate trying circumstances

Pity: feeling of sympathy or sadness because somebody else is in trouble or pain or the capacity to feel this; regrettable thing; mercy; expression of sympathy or regret; to feel pity for somebody's pain or trouble

Solidity: reliable

Steadfastness: firm and unwavering in purpose, loyalty, or resolve; fixed, firmly fixed, constant

Tenderness: with gentle feeling; kind and sympathetic

Tolerance: acceptance of different views; putting up with someone or something irritating or otherwise unpleasant; ability to endure hardship; ability to remain unaffected; allowance made for deviation; ability to withstand extremes

Understanding: ability to grasp a meaning; ability to perceive and explain the meaning; interpretation of something; mutual comprehension; knowledge of another's nature; sympathetically aware; able to know something

His Mercy Endures Forever
Psalm 136:1

Bibliography

The Contemporary English Version. Nashville, TN: Thomas Nelson, 1995.
The New American Bible: Revised Edition. New Jersey: Catholic Book, 2011.
O'Day, Gail R., and David Petersen, eds. *The Access Bible: New Revised Standard Version with the Apocryphal/Deuterocanonical Books, Updated Edition.* New York: Oxford University Press, 2011.
Peterson, Eugene H., and William Griffin, trans. *The Message: Catholic/Ecumenical Edition, The Bible in Contemporary Language.* Chicago, IL; ACTA, 2013.

Recent Books by Mark G. Boyer

Nature Spirituality: Praying with Wind, Water, Earth, Fire

A Spirituality of Ageing

Weekday Saints: Reflections on Their Scriptures

Human Wholeness: A Spirituality of Relationship

A Simple Systematic Mariology

Praying Your Way through Luke's Gospel and the Acts of the Apostles

An Abecedarian of Animal Spirit Guides: Spiritual Growth through Reflections on Creatures

Overcome with Paschal Joy: Chanting through Lent and Easter—Daily Reflections with Familiar Hymns

Taking Leave of Your Home: Moving in the Peace of Christ

An Abecedarian of Sacred Trees: Spiritual Growth through Reflections on Woody Plants

Divine Presence: Elements of Biblical Theophanies

Fruit of the Vine: A Biblical Spirituality of Wine

Names for Jesus: Reflections for Advent and Christmas

Talk to God and Listen to the Casual Reply: Experiencing the Spirituality of John Denver

Recent Books by Mark G. Boyer

Christ Our Passover Has Been Sacrificed: A Guide through Paschal Mystery Spirituality—Mystical Theology in The Roman Missal

Rosary Primer: The Prayers, The Mysteries, and the New Testament

From Contemplation to Action: The Spiritual Process of Divine Discernment Using Elijah and Elisha as Models

Love Addict

All Things Mary: Honoring the Mother of God—An Anthology of Marian Reflections

Shhh! The Sound of Sheer Silence: A Biblical Spirituality that Transforms

What is Born of the Spirit is Spirit: A Biblical Spirituality of Spirit

Very Short Reflections—for Advent and Christmas, Lent and Easter, Ordinary Time, and Saints—through the Liturgical Year

Living Parables: Today's Versions

My Life of Ministry, Writing, Teaching, and Traveling: The Autobiography of an Old Mines Missionary

300 Years of the French in Old Mines: A Narrative History of the Oldest Village in Missouri

Journey into God: Spiritual Reflections for Travelers

Monthly Entries for the Spiritual but not Religious through the Year: Texts, Reflections, Journal/Meditations, and Prayers for the Spiritual but not Religious

The Shelbydog Chronicles by Shelby Cole as Recorded by Mark G. Boyer: A Novel

Four Catholic Pioneers in Missouri: Lamarque, Kenrick, Fox, and Hogan: Irish Missionaries and Their Supporter

Smothered with Inexhaustible Mercy: An Anthology of Poems

Spirituality for the Solitary: A Handbook for Those Who Live Alone

Seasons of Biblical Spirituality: Spring, Summer, Autumn, Winter

RECENT BOOKS BY MARK G. BOYER

Biblical Names for God: An Abecedarian Anthology of Spiritual Reflections for Anytime

More Shelbydog Chronicles: Reflections on a Dog's Life by Her Friend, Knowing Your Pet

www.ingramcontent.com/pod-product-compliance
Lightning Source LLC
Chambersburg PA
CBHW050813160426
43192CB00010B/1745